# ABOUT THE AUTHORS

Barrington Orwell maintained an incomparable reputation in three-and-a-half decades of almost perpetual employment until his tragic death in an unexplained contrabassoon accident early in 2013.

His work as a conductor was without parallel, and critical reaction was copious and unrestrained:

'...Conductor Barrington Orwell was not able [sic]...' *South Yorkshire Bugle*

'...achieved sounds undreamed of by the composer...' *Berkhamsted Gazette*

'Orwell's conducting...took the art to a new level...' *Süddeutscher Blatt*

'...quite simply beyond words...' *Torbay Gleaner*

'Incredible...' *Audience member*

'The Beethoven...was...fast...' *Leamington Herald*

'I think it safe to say that in thirty years of concert-going I have yet to see a display of conducting to compare with Orwell's stupefying effort...' *South West Cotswold and District Newsletter*

L EV PARIKIAN was born. After a tediously lengthy period of growing, he became an adult.

He spends a lot of time standing in front of people waving his arms in the hope that sounds will materialise.

He also spends a lot of time staring at a computer screen in the hope that words will materialise.

The production of this book is therefore a triumph of hope over experience.

He lives in London with his [redacted], [redacted], and three domesticated (and, rest assured, entirely neutralised) [redacted].

He has never been to Uzbekistan.

This book started life as a series of articles in Classical Music magazine. Both the title and some excerpts from those articles appear with permission.

www.classicalmusicmagazine.org

# *Waving, Not Drowning*

Barrington Orwell

Lev Parikian

ISBN-13: 978-1484114506
ISBN-10: 1484114507

To all musicians and conductors,

especially the few who are both.

# CONTENTS

# AUTHORS' NOTES

THE GREAT TEACHER, Professor Etwas Ruhiger, was fond of saying: 'Zere is nussink in life zat is not viz condectink to be doink.'

How true.

And so, to facilitate understanding of what follows, the first part of the book (or *amuse-bouche*, if you will, and even if you won't) will deal with some of my influences in music and in life. I thank them from the depth of my being for their part in my formation as a quasi-coherent conductor and passable excuse for a human being, but stress with the utmost vehemence that none of what follows is their fault.

The main course is a heartier affair, and consists of my thoughts on the craft of conducting. It is an entirely personal view, and should not be thought of as prescriptive.

Where I say 'Do not', feel free to; where I say 'Let yourself', feel free not to; where I say 'The alert conductor', feel free to dissociate yourself from that hypothetical breed.

And, crucially, where I say 'he', you can take it as read that I mean 'he or she' but am too lazy to write it.

Most of all, it is my devout wish that, after reading this book, you will be able to stand in front of an orchestra and not make them worse.

I am indebted to my amanuensis Lev Parikian, whose indefatigable efforts and eye for detail have ensured that this book will reach the printers as free from errors as posible.

*Barrington Orwell*

*South Mimms Service Station, January 2013*

**B**ARRINGTON ORWELL was one of a kind: a musician of extreme individuality, and a conductor of sterling and largely misunderstood credentials. It is often said, when talking about conductors, that any fool can drive a Rolls-Royce, but just see how that fool fares when put behind the wheel of a Trabant. The latter was Barry's milieu, and he thrived in it. The sounds he wrought from a simplified arrangement of *The Pink Panther Theme* had to be heard to be believed.

In a different life, perhaps he would have achieved more widespread recognition. But the music profession is a cruel mistress, and even Barry must have become weighed down by the tell-tale signs of a relationship turned sour: the infidelities, the lies, the anniversary meal congealing on the bitter plate of despair.

I knew him for the last ten years of his life, our paths first crossing at a conducting seminar where I was giving a talk on 'The Cause and Effect of Involuntary Rubato'. His excoriating dissection of my lecture in the bar afterwards was brutal but kindly; his insistence that I dine as his guest that evening typical of a man for whom mere difference of opinion was no barrier to friendship.

Over the next few years we spent many hours in avid discussion, our passionate discourse often fuelled by a bottle or two of Schlockenbinter Grünger Feldkopfliner or one of the many other delights from the

Pandora's box that was his extensive and brilliantly chosen cellar. These conversations went on into the night, covering every aspect of music and in particular the craft of conducting, a discipline that Barry (as he, with atypical ambivalence, both loved and hated to be called) found mysterious and bewildering.

What is the optimum podium size? What exactly did Mahler mean by the marking 'Sehr sehr, aber nicht zu sehr'? Pencils: 2B or...

Well, you get the idea.

It was during these late night chats that the plan for this book was hatched. 'Tell it like it really is' became our motto, and Barry applied his formidable brain to the task with his customary dedication, fearlessness and disregard for punctuality. I acted, for the most part, as secretary, trying to catch the emanations of his quicksilver brain before they withered and were lost forever.

At 3am one morning earlier this year, Barry squinted across the kitchen table in my general direction and made a cryptic declaration, the gist of which, once I'd extracted it from some earthy comments about my ancestry, seemed to be that our project was closed.

At any rate, further wisdom was not forthcoming, and I set about the task of collating the wealth of material he had flung at me over the previous few months.

Then, five days later, came the hammer blow.

Barry was found in the instrument store at his local music service headquarters, apparently the victim of a freak contrabassoon accident. Legal reasons prevent me from going into further details at the time of going to press.

Needless to say, the void caused by Barry's loss was incalculable. But although he was gone, my task remained the same: assemble his thoughts into some sort of coherent order. His retelling of his early years, while at times rambling and incomprehensible, was nonetheless riddled with what appeared to be fascinating observations about the unfathomable mysteries of conducting. And when it came to insight into the craft, Barry was second to none. If at times his views contradicted each other, this ambiguity was offset by an uncanny ability to find the pith at the heart of the subject.

It was my job to take the pith and pass it on to you.

I have done my best to represent his views as accurately as possible—if I have failed to do so, the fault is mine. By the same token, if I can take the credit for anything, it is merely the contribution of a competent mechanic assembling an engine from the blueprint of a master designer. The creative spark was all Barry's. May he rest in peace.

*Lev Parikian*
*West Norwood, March 2013*

# Introduction

YOU STAND ON THE podium, finest Armani caress-
ing your skin. The scent of Hugo Boss aftershave
tickles your nostrils. You've chosen it specially—Hugo
Boss is a Mahler kind of perfume. Calvin Klein was for
the first half, its manly brusqueness, almost bullying
but just backing off at the right moment, perfectly
matched to the lean muscularity of Beethoven. But
Hugo is subtler, more complex. He puts you in the
mood, does Hugo.

The applause has died down and now there is ex-
pectancy in the air. You bring your focus to the matter
in hand.

Mahler.

Ah, Gustav. Gustle. Gussie. Every conductor's
soulmate. The one composer whose music could be said
to be written for the man at the front. It's almost as if
he's woven the choreography into the music, every
shake, lunge, heave and grunt as integral to it as the
notes themselves.

But not every conductor understands it the way you
do. Your bond with this music is infrangible. Themes,
sub-themes, counterpoint, harmony, rhythm, texture,
the very fabric of the music itself—they are weaved
inextricably into the core of your being. Your interpretation is imbued with such musical honesty, such
(dare you say it) humanity, that to call it an 'interpretation' is to do it an injustice. It's as if Gus, Gussing-
ton, Sir Gustavo von der Mahlerstein himself has
tattooed it into your cerebral cortex with his own
spindly hand, perhaps in a seedy backstreet tattoo par-
lour in the Vienna that was his home, and where you
spent such enjoyable years (the Sachertorte! The Kaf-
fee! The Kuchen!) researching, living, breathing, ab-
sorbing the master's spirit.

And now, at last, your time has come. From this
moment forward the world will know that the spirit of

Gustav shines like a beacon once more, in the form of your dedicated, talented, hard-working-but-painfully-modest self.

There's only one problem.

You don't know how to begin.

The music is perfectly formed in your head; if only you could say the same about the upbeat you need to give so the musicians can begin to realise your vision.

You hesitate. The orchestra, like a thoroughbred used to a multiple Derby-winning jockey but suddenly in the not-so-tender care of a spotty stable boy, senses your fear. All is lost.

Mahler, not for the first time, dies a long and painful death.

It's a common enough problem. Many is the aspiring conductor whose promising career has been—how to put this tactfully?—shafted like an in-heat antelope on the veldt for want of a decent *Auftakt*.

And even if you negotiate the beginning without catastrophe, what then? Tempo, phrasing, dynamics, balance, ebb and flow, tension and release, accelerandi, ritardandi, recitatives, accompaniment, programming, player management...all the way through to pudding wine choices and beyond; the responsibilities facing the modern Maestro take the breath away.

It makes you wonder why anyone would want to do it.

But don't worry. Be not afeared. Help is at hand.

This book is...well, what is this book? Who is it for?

This book is for everyone.

Maybe you're the avid classical music fan who wants to delve yet deeper into the warp and weft of the art form that you've adored since your Uncle Albert dandled you on his knee, humming along to a scratched 78 of Sir Adrian Boult's recording of the *Overture to La Gazza Ladra*, his bristly moustache tickling your ear and the words 'This is the kind of thing, eh? None of that modern rot' on his port-infused breath.

Or perhaps you're a complete novice, whose only involvement with Western Art Music thus far has been a drunken karaoke rendition of *Nessun Dorma* at the office party and the Katherine Jenkins album given to you one Christmas by a well-meaning aunt. You're determined to better yourself, and not just to impress Sandra, although her reaction when you put that Miles Davis album on makes you think she might be susceptible to the kind of bloke who knows a bit about music. You've toyed with the idea of learning an instrument, but you have neighbours, and didn't Charlie take up the piano and tell you how terribly hard it was? Far easier, surely, to learn about conducting—and terribly impressive, too.

At the other end of the spectrum, maybe you're a disillusioned orchestral musician, fed up with the man (or woman—let's not pretend that it is only men who are egotistical maniacs) whose self-glorifying antics and impenetrable gestures do so much to blight your daily working life. You're determined to prove them all wrong—conductors can be down-to-earth, honest musicians with functional upbeats and an unaffected style; they can be generous, humble and genuinely engaged in the craft for the service of the music. Perhaps you can be the first of them. You can certainly do better than the one they had in last week—what a charlatan! (NB: 'the one they had in last week' was always awful, no matter how good you secretly thought he was.)

I humbly submit that there is something in here for all of you. If you learn just one thing from this book, whether it be the best speed for *Nimrod* when played in a muddy field outside Saffron Walden or the correct amount to tip a stage-door Johnny in Caracas, I will have, in part at least, fulfilled my duty.

# PART ONE

# INFLUENCES

# [1]

# *My Father*

I AM OFTEN asked 'When did you know you were going to be a conductor?'

I may be mistaken, but I have a distinct memory that the midwife's efforts to coax the first stertorous breaths from my infant lungs were woefully lacking in rhythm. Then, in the Intensive Care Unit, my efforts to make the other children wail in tune, or at least in synchronisation, were sadly misinterpreted by the doctors as being in some way related to a desire for my mother's milk.

If there was a clue to be found in my ancestry as to my future career, then it certainly wasn't to be found easily. Music played no more a part in the lives of my parents than subtlety and humility do in Donald Trump's.

In our modern and 'enlightened' world, music is hard to avoid. Entire populations are encouraged to display their 'talent' on prime-time television as if merely opening your mouth and allowing the spirit to guide you is enough to send the audience into whooping paroxysms of orgasmic delight (which, to be fair, it often is); musical 'education' consists of little more than thrusting a set of jingles into an unsuspecting child's hand, posting the results on YouTube with the title 'Santa's Little Helper—Amazing Talent!' and daring the world to contradict you; and no office's annual calendar is complete without the ritual humiliation of the 'Karaoke Night'—an appalling monstrosity in which ordinary members of the public compete to find which of them can execute the bloodiest atrocity on the popular music of the day.

Music assaults us everywhere and everywhen, from the G♭ major chord that greets us on booting up our computer, through the incessant butchery of the telephone hold Muzak, all the way to ghastly novelty items such as the Christmas-carol-playing toilet roll holder or the musical condom and beyond.

In the Northamptonshire of the early 1960s it was much easier to be music-free, and it was to this ideal that my parents seemed to aspire. More amusical than unmusical, they had no television ('Satan's evil chest'), and the wireless was used only for news bulletins and *Mrs Dale's Diary*. My father's idea of an evening's entertainment was to read to us from the volume of

Lamb's *Tales of Shakespeare* that lurked heavily on
the front room bookshelf. It would no more have occurred to them to go to a concert, had there existed
such a luxury in the cultural outpost we called home,
than it would occur to Katie Price to translate the
works of Marcel Proust into Danish.

The only time this musical vacuum was breached
was on Sundays. Community singing was different.
Every Sunday the three of us would tramp up the hill
and take the same pew in the village church. And every
Sunday my parents would 'sing' along with the rest of
the congregation.

Mr. Archbold, the organist, was a gentle, bespecta-
cled man. The top of his bald head was just visible
from where I sat, and I used to thrill to the sight of it
bobbing up and down very nearly in time with the music. He had been organist-in-residence at St. Ethel-
burga's church for some fifty years, and yet for all the
wealth of experience that he brought to the rôle, he
never quite came to grips with such musical subtleties
as rhythm, meter or key signatures. As a result he gave
the congregation few clues as to where the singing
should begin and end. On many occasions, indeed, it
was not readily apparent which hymn we should be
singing. The resultant noise was one that would have
excited the great musical experimenter Charles Ives,
but few others.

*Waving, Not Drowning*

This uncertainty had little effect on my parents. While my mother mewed apologetically to my left, it was my father, on the other side, who caught the eye and, more irresistibly, the ear. His approach to a hymn was to seize it by the scruff of the neck and shake it until it fell to the floor, spluttering and coughing up blood, its will broken beyond any human help. The sight and sound of him, hair Brylcreemed to the point of drowning, collar cutting into his wobbling neck, and ruddy cheeks glowing with exertion, bellowing *Come, and Let Us Sweetly Join* in a manner that brooked no argument, will remain with me to my dying day. The empty pews around us, in a relatively well-attended church, told their own story.

Away from the church, it was as if music didn't exist. So if the home environment was musically barren, how was the seed of my love for it sown?

Take a bow, Uncle Ted.

# [2]

# *Uncle Ted*

MY MOTHER'S ONLY SISTER Vera had married, according to my father, beneath her.

This conclusion was based not so much on social status—my father was not well-placed to stand in judgement of others in this department—as on an irrational distaste for what he called 'poncery'. Included in this category were such heinous sins as sherry, cravats and thick shag pile carpets, all of which made up a small part of Uncle Ted's vicious armoury of dandified twaddle.

Visits to Ted and Vera's were infrequently and unwillingly undertaken. At Easter and Christmas, and once in the summer holidays, we would travel the fifty miles or so to Wisbech in the family Ford Zephyr, my father muttering under his breath with ill-concealed hatred.

'They never come to us, do they? No, Mr. La-di-da wouldn't sully himself by getting into a motor car. He'd rather swan around in his flippin' cravat drinking sherry than go to the trouble of seeing how real people live.'

'Now now, Arthur. It's very kind of them to invite us. And to be fair, they've never come to us because we've never asked them.'

The expression 'to be fair' was my mother's stock-in-trade. A mild-mannered woman, though by no means weak of will, she spent a fair deal of her time, in public and private, softening the blow of my father's imprudent and readily-shared opinions. It is from her that I have inherited what patience I have; from my father, the unshakeable conviction of being in the right that is an essential part of any conductor's personality.

'Well, just don't expect me to engage in conversation.' My father was gripping the steering wheel so tightly that his knuckles turned white. 'I intend to sit in the corner and get quietly drunk.'

'Not too drunk, I hope. Knowing our luck, we'll get stopped and you'll be given one of those breath tests on the way home.'

'And I tell you, if he's playing that racket when we get there we're turning straight back round and going home.'

'Now you're just being silly.'

14

'That racket' was music. Specifically, classical music. More specifically, nineteenth- and early twentieth-century Romantic music. Brahms, Schumann, Dvořák, Bruckner, Elgar, Mahler. All played on pristine state-of-the-art equipment at a high volume. I suppose I was about eight when the sounds emanating from Uncle Ted's Bang & Olufsen morphed from the perplexing into something irresistibly arresting. In the interests of politeness, Ted would turn down the volume once we were established in the front room of their more-spacious-than-ours house. My father, sitting in the most uncomfortable chair in the room, nursed his glass of sherry, his feet awkwardly perched on the thick salmon-pink carpet, and answered Uncle Ted's conversational gambits with a mixture of sullen grunts and non-committal assenting sounds. My mother chatted to her sister on the other side of the room. I, the only child present, moved closer to the speakers so as not to lose contact with the mysterious and entrancing sound that was coming from them.

While I sat cross-legged, immersed in the music, I saw my father's discomfort as he did his best to make small talk with a man with whom he had absolutely nothing in common. He fiddled with his sherry glass, trying to draw attention to the fact that it was empty without being actively rude.

'Busy time of year?'

'Hmm.'

'I suppose you'll be doing the usual for your summer holidays?'

'Grrff.'

'He likes music, then, the lad?'

'Mrrggll.'

'Look at him, he's absolutely buried in it. Miles away.'

'Mmphm.'

'He can borrow one of these, if he wants. Take it away and listen to it on the gramophone at home.'

'Don't have one.'

'What's that? Don't have a home or don't have a gramophone?'

Uncle Ted was enjoying himself. He'd known my father for years, and was fully aware of the situation.

'Gramophone.'

'Well that's no good, is it? You should get him one. It's the stuff of life, music is. Can't have a house without music, can you?'

But we could, and did.

After lunch I sat, waiting for the moment when I could get down from the formal dining table, and plucking up courage to ask Uncle Ted if I could go back into the front room and listen to more music.

He was way ahead of me.

'Now then, why don't we go next door and put on some more of that Mahler?'

So Uncle Ted and I went back into the front room and spent the rest of the afternoon in our own world, impervious to the stultifying conversation being inflicted on my father in the dining room. While we listened, Uncle Ted told me something about the lives of the great composers, his narrative peppered with fascinating and unbelievable facts. I discovered years later that they were indeed unbelievable for the simple reason that they weren't facts at all, but had been made up on the spot by Uncle Ted to keep me entertained.

'Now Mahler, he was an interesting one. Allergic to broccoli. Nearly died of it.'

Or: 'Brahms and Tchaikovsky were the only great composers who had wooden legs.'

Or: 'You wouldn't think it, to look at him, but Bruckner owned twenty-six cats, one for each letter of the alphabet.'

Or: 'It was Beethoven, of course, who cut off his own ear.'

'Is that Beethoven?' I asked, pointing at the photograph on the sleeve of an album called 'My Favourite Overtures'. The photograph showed a man in a smart grey suit staring gimlet-eyed into the camera. His beard was sharp enough to be banned under the Offensive Weapons Act.

17

Uncle Ted laughed.

'That? Oh heck no, that's Sir Thomas Beecham.'

'Who's he?'

'He's a conductor.'

'What's a conductor?'

And so it began.

As he explained the rôle of the conductor, a seed was planted in my brain.

Imagine, I thought, standing in the middle of this.

'Does the conductor play an instrument?'

'No lad, he plays the whole orchestra. And he carries a big white stick which he waves around in time with the music, and all the musicians have to do what he says.' A cloud of alcohol fumes billowed towards me as he leaned forward and tapped me on the knee. 'And he earns thousands and thousands of pounds a year.'

Sold. In truth, he had me at 'big white stick.'

IT'S EASY TO FIND significant moments in retrospect. 'In that one act of cruelty the seeds were sown—the decades of Pol Pot's tyranny can be laid at the door of his primary school teacher.' That kind of thing.

But the truth is more nebulous than that.

So while the details of that afternoon seem clear to me, it is much more likely that they're an amalgam, that I have conflated my memories of several visits to Uncle Ted into one pivotal event.

One thing is certain: those visits transformed me.

Uncle Ted's tastes were not broad. He didn't listen to string quartets or piano music, and opera was a closed book to him.

'They ruin the music with all that singing,' he told me once with a pained expression.

No, it was orchestral music he liked. And the richer and lusher the better. The amateur psychologist will try, as I did in later years, to analyse these tastes, to see in them a necessary antidote to his dry working life and sterile marriage.

But I think he just liked the sound the orchestra made.

Mahler featured prominently, of course. Brahms was another favourite. I have a vague recollection of an unsuccessful foray into the murky world of Hindemith, who I suppose had become briefly fashionable.

We didn't go there again.

Nor did we visit the likes of Stravinsky or Britten, and the Second Viennese School received no more than passing scorn from Uncle Ted.

'If that's music, then I'm the Queen Mother.'

Even I could see that he was not.

There arose a sort of impasse between me and my father. I wanted to visit Ted and Vera more often, because of the music; he, for the same reason, wanted to visit them less. And my pleadings for a gramophone went unheeded. So my musical diet remained frustratingly irregular—a general famine, punctuated by a triannual feast.

The next Christmas, emboldened by three glasses of Liebfraumilch, Uncle Ted locked horns with my father.

'You really should get a gramophone, you know, Arthur. All the rage, they are. And you can listen to spoken word too.'

'If I want the spoken word I can have a conversation.'

And that was that.

Despite this encouragement (or possibly because of it), my father steadfastly refused to entertain the possibility, leaving me to fend for myself. Carefully hoarding my weekly pocket money, I worked out that I would be able to save up enough for a gramophone in just twelve years. Of course, I would then have to start saving again in order to afford anything to play on it, but in this I was prepared to play the long game.

Luckily fate intervened in the form of Uncle Ted's mother. Her untimely death while changing a light bulb was unfortunate for her and traumatic for Uncle Ted, but life-changing for me. Uncle Ted, her only child, inherited everything, his father having died some years previously, a victim of all thirteen volumes of his much-loved Oxford English Dictionary, a faultily fitted shelf and the immutable nature of the laws of gravity. This macabre coincidence might have led Uncle Ted into a life of caution, but strangely it had the opposite effect, and he became notorious in his later years for taking on ever more risky household tasks with a glint in his eye, as if confronting Fate head on and saying 'Come on you bugger, come and have me and all.'

Amongst the items left by Uncle Ted's mother was a portable gramophone, (or 'record player' as it was by now known) which Uncle Ted passed on to me the next Christmas, to looks of dark menace from my father, who insisted that I carry it to the car myself, along with the 'starter pack' of Brahms Symphonies that Uncle Ted had given me as a Christmas present.

So began a two-year war between me and my father. I listened to my records as often as I could; he told me to 'Turn that racket down'. I sat hunched over the record player, volume turned as low as it would go without dwindling to complete silence, listening to my latest acquisition from the public library; he hovered on the landing, waiting for me to give him reason to vent his spleen.

I wouldn't go so far as to suggest that my father secretly liked music, but I think he may at the very least

have been fascinated by the strange sounds that capti-
vated me so entirely. But there was no way that he was
going to show any sign of yielding. That would have
been a display of weakness. I, for my part, was addict-
ed. My repertoire broadened, encompassing Bach, Mozart, Haydn, string quartets, piano music, and many
other composers and genres untouched by Uncle Ted.
I devoured music with the insatiable appetite other
children showed for sweets. Each fix merely heightened the desire for the next. And so the stalemate continued, with no end in sight.

And then Miss Lovejoy's breasts happened.

# [3]

# *Aurelia Lovejoy*

RETURNING FROM SCHOOL one autumn afternoon, I paused on the front step, disturbed by something different. The air, normally filled with the imperfect silence of modern life, was punctured.

There were sounds. Tinkling, melodious sounds. Well, melodious to my ears, at least.

I turned round, trying to locate the source.

Outside No. 36, over the road, was parked a car I hadn't seen before. A red Triumph Vitesse. It stood out amongst the drab commuter cars on our street as a daring statement, a splash of glamour in a relentlessly grey area.

It was from behind the Triumph that the sounds were coming. I crossed the road in a trance. Had there been a twelve-tonne juggernaut thundering towards me, poised to crush the life out of my now eleven-year-old body, I wouldn't have noticed. I was drawn to the sounds as inexorably as an alcoholic to Happy Hour.

I pressed my nose against the window of No. 36. There, in the front room, was a piano. It was being played by a lady. That the lady was lissom, elegant and beautiful was something that would become apparent to me in due course, but all I saw and heard at that moment was the piano.

'What are you doing, you perv?'

I snapped my head round towards the voice. To my astonishment I saw its owner standing on the doorstep a couple of yards to my left. Kevin 'Chinese' Burn: bane of my life, class bully, and one-boy cultural vacuum.

'What...?'

'Stop perving my piano teacher. I saw you.'

'But...I was...'

It occurred to me, just in time, that perhaps it would be better to admit lechery than the real reason for my hypnotised state.

'Mind you,' he said, pressing the door bell, 'can't blame you.' And he made the universal male sign denoting attractive mammaries. 'Phwoar, eh?'

The lady stopped playing the piano and got up to answer the door. Trying to gather my senses, I attempted a riposte.

'What are you doing having piano lessons?'

'What, are you off your rocker or summat? Any excuse to get close to Miss Titsjoy. Oh hello, Miss Lovejoy,' he continued, easing into good-little-boy-come-for-his-piano-lesson mode with the practised ease of a true master, 'I hope I'm not too early.'

'No, not at all, Kevin. I hope you managed to find it easily. The new place isn't quite as cosy as the old one, but I'm sure...'

Her voice disappeared as she walked down the hall. Giving me one last leer, Chinese Burn followed Miss Lovejoy into her house. I turned slowly away and crossed the road, lost in thought. All my pleading for piano lessons had come to nothing, and now Chinese Burn, a boy whose sole musical talent was his ability to burp something that sounded like the national anthem, was having piano lessons and I wasn't.

Blinded by the injustice of life, I stumbled through the front door and up the stairs to my room, where I sought solace in Beethoven's *Archduke Trio* and the latest issue of *Musical Quarterly*.

F ACED WITH THE DAILY torture of hearing a piano to which I would have no access, I resorted to the technique beloved of children all over the world since time immemorial: incessant whining.

'I'll practise every day. You wouldn't have to listen to it. I can do it at school, in break. I asked Mr. Summerscales.'

My father opened the front door to put out the milk bottles. At the same moment the door opposite opened, and out stepped Miss Lovejoy, wearing a checked miniskirt and short orange leather jacket.

The instant my father saw her, our house leaped to the head of the country's drool production league table.

'Dad...'

'Eh? What?' He lingered on the doorstep, nearly tripping over his own tongue as Miss Lovejoy leant over the car's soft top. She unclasped it and rolled it back as if auditioning for a rôle in a Carry On film. Reluctantly my father turned his attention back to me. 'Yes, well...I don't know, lad...you see, it's an expensive business, playing the piano, and time-consuming, too. I suppose you'd have to practise a lot, wouldn't you?'

'I was just saying...I can do it at sch–'

'But on the other hand, I suppose it would be very convenient, and you do seem to have your heart set on it.'

'Well...'

'Tell you what, son. I'm not making any promises, but it does seem a shame to waste the opportunity. I mean, she's just on our doorstep, isn't she? And you've been pestering me for ages...let's go and have a chat to her and see what it will entail. No promises, mind.'

Emboldened and pinkening, he called out to Miss Lovejoy.

'Excuse me!'

She paused, one leg in the car, the other on the pavement, her hand on the roof, face upturned in polite enquiry.

My father's confidence disappeared as miraculously as an odd sock in a tumble dryer. He stood holding the empty milk bottles, suddenly ridiculous, a plain middle-aged man out of his depth.

'Yes...well, hello...I, er...we...er...'

'We were wondering if I could have some piano lessons.'

I wasn't going to have my only chance scuppered by my father's fecklessness. I walked across the road to find Miss Lovejoy looking at me assessingly.

'I don't see why not,' she said.

Her voice seemed to me unnaturally low, lower than it had been when she was talking to Chinese Burn. I was dimly aware of my father melting by my side.

As I talked to Miss Lovejoy and we made arrangements for my first lesson, I was in two minds.

On the one hand, I was delighted that I had got my way. On the other, dismayed to see my father in such a transparently delirious state. I had a vague notion that this was something to do with sex, a concept as alien to me at that time as a Bugatti Veyron would be to the pygmy tribesmen of the Congo.

And I was also aware that the focus of my father's desire was Miss Lovejoy's bosom. I'd gleaned, from Chinese Burn's lascivious and precocious taunts, that bosoms, and specifically Miss Lovejoy's bosoms, were something to be cherished. If the exact reason for this was beyond my pre-pubescent understanding, the fact of their desirability to my father was obvious. From that day in September 1965, he could, in truth, look at little else until June 1972, when they would be taken away from him with brutal finality.

Miss Lovejoy's breasts would, in time, come to gain a more personal significance to me, but at this point they were symbols of an insoluble dilemma: because of them, I could have piano lessons, and as such they were an undeniable force for good; but they were also responsible for the ongoing public humiliation of my father, a process of which he seemed blissfully unaware.

For now, I was content enough to have an opportunity to develop my burning desire to make music. I had grown to depend on my listening sessions as an antidote to the mundanity of my academic and social lives. But now I wanted more. I wanted to make the sounds. I remembered what Uncle Ted had told me that day—'he plays the orchestra...waves a white stick in time to the music...thousands and thousands of pounds...'—and it occurred to me that this was an entirely desirable way to spend one's time. But I had no idea of how I might find an orchestra, nor how I could possibly persuade them to let me conduct them.

I did, of course, wave my arms around in time to the sounds emanating from my cherished record player. But while this was initially satisfying in a superficial way, even I, a callow eleven-year-old, could tell that it was not the real thing. Apart from anything else, if I needed a wee or stopped waving my arms for any other reason, the music carried on. I wasn't responsible for the sound—I was merely pleasuring myself alongside it.

So this opportunity to make music with my own hands was exactly what I had been waiting for, and I threw myself into it with all the enthusiasm of a starving cat in a mouse colony.

Miss Lovejoy was delighted by my progress.

'We are a quick learner, aren't we?' she breathed after I had played, with some aplomb, an elementary piece she had given me just two weeks before. She leaned across to point something out, and I caught a whiff of her scent. Behind me, my father shifted slightly in the armchair from which he supervised my lessons. He had insisted that he be there at every one, claiming that he did it solely for my welfare.

'Not right, your being in there by yourself. Nothing against Miss Lovejoy, but that's the way it is,' he'd told me one evening.

Miss Lovejoy, for her part, had no objection to my father's presence. Far from it.

'I must say it's rare for a father to take such a keen interest in his son's musical development,' she husked. 'Do you play yourself?'

She gave him a weird look, of the kind it would take me a couple of years to understand.

My father's mumbled reply left us none the wiser. I decided to help out.

'We've never had any music in the house. Father hates it.'

The red of my father's cheeks deepened, now accompanied by a flash of anger in the eyes. He still seemed unable to string together a coherent sentence in Miss Lovejoy's presence, however, which was probably just as well.

'Deary me, I can't imagine that! A life without music!' She twinkled at my father. 'We'll have to educate you, Mr. Busse. No use you living out your years untouched by man's greatest gift.'

If I'd had a marshmallow handy, I could have cooked it simply by taking it out of my pocket and holding it within a couple of feet of my father's cheeks.

Miss Lovejoy's intervention put my father in a pickle, from which he sought to extract himself over the next few days. The strength of his desire to ingratiate himself with her overwhelmed his undeniably potent antipathy towards music. So, clearly hating every second, he joined me in my listening sessions, sitting on the hard chair in the corner of my room while I lay on the bed. I was going through a period of discovery, the music of Igor Stravinsky having exerted a stranglehold on my imagination. My father, unable to sit and just listen, interrupted the delicate atmosphere of concentration every few seconds with questions.

'That instrument, is that a trumpet?'

'Bassoon.'

'Oh. Ah.'

Pause.

'This bit, what's it about again?'

'Stravinsky said that it represents the awakening of nature.'

'Oh.'

We listened a bit longer, while I tried to send anti-talking vibes across the room.

'Not much of a tune, is there?'

'That's not really the idea.'

'Oh.'

I should have been grateful for his interest—instead, I just wanted him to shut up.

I became aware of a pained expression on his face.

'How long does it last again?'

'About half an hour.'

This information was received with a barely stifled moan.

'Have you got anything a bit more...you know...nice? Maybe something with some words? Some singing?'

I was seized with mischief.

'Well there's Wagner.'

'Really? What's that then?'

'Oh you'll love it, Dad. Lots of words.'

I took the needle off *The Rite of Spring*, reached for the boxed set of *Das Rheingold* that I had been saving for the weekend, and prepared to plunge my father into a deep pit of misery.

WE SETTLED INTO A ROUTINE. I played some music, my father hated it, I squirmed with private delight.

I only discovered after his death that he was secretly pleased and proud that I had let him into my world. And, more to the point, he was able to hold his own in conversations with Miss Lovejoy—or 'Aurelia', as she soon came to be known.

In spite of the simmering sexual tension between them, I managed to focus my energies on actually learning the piano. In this endeavour I was successful. Miss Lovejoy was a good and diligent teacher, and I quickly became her star pupil, much to the blistering chagrin of Chinese Burn. My progress was swift, and it soon became clear to Miss Lovejoy that I was a candidate for more specialised musical education. In July 1967 I sat, and passed, the Music Scholarship examination for St. Umbrage's College.

If I owe my parents for bringing me into the world and raising me, and Uncle Ted for introducing me to music, the greatest debt is to Miss Aurelia Lovejoy. It was she who first enabled me to express my love of music in a practical way. She also, one memorable and sadly unrepeated afternoon a few years later, rendered tuition in a subject that was not, strictly speaking, within her remit. I may owe her more for that act of kindness than for all the music lessons put together.

# [4]

# David Branston

S T. UMBRAGE'S IS A PUBLIC SCHOOL of the old-fashioned type, set in several acres of rambling grounds. Its main buildings impose themselves on the surrounding playing fields from a privileged position on the top of a hill, their austere grandeur designed to intimidate generations of cowering children into a semblance of academic effort.

Although it was set up in the 1600s for the children of the poor, such noble ambitions have long been cast aside, and only a few non-fee-paying places are available each year for students of high academic, sporting or musical potential. In truth, academic and sporting standards at St. Umbrage's in the 1960s were not high, but it was the music I was there for. While there were other schools offering music scholarships, they were mostly further afield, and St. Umbrage's had the crucial advantage that Miss Lovejoy was 'acquainted with' the Head of Music.

She'd been optimistic about my chances of success in the scholarship exam.

'Believe me, I think they'll take quite a shine to you,' she said with a knowing smile.

My father was less sanguine.

'Bloody waste of time. What's wrong with the local school? They do music there.'

I tried to explain, but I might as well have lectured an aardvark on the basic principles of quantum physics. For all his efforts, inspired by Miss Lovejoy's *embonpoint*, my father and music remained almost total strangers, forever condemned to nod awkwardly at each other over the flourishing garden hedge of incomprehension.

In the exam itself, I had been required to do little more than play my set pieces on the piano and answer a few basic musical questions, as well as pass a painfully simple aural test.

The Head of Music, Mr. Branston, glossed over my lack of a second instrument, which I had understood to be a mandatory requirement.

'I'm sure you'll catch up very quickly. Perhaps you could take up the violin or cello when...if you're accepted. Aurel–... Miss Lovejoy tells me you're a fast learner.'

'She's a very good teacher, sir.'

He looked at the floor, cheeks slightly pink.

'Indeed so.'

And that was that. I was in.

L IFE AT ST. UMBRAGE'S quickly divided itself into two parts: music and everything else. I tried to fill as much of my time as possible with the former, while devising ever more ingenious ploys to avoid the latter.

I submitted myself to violin lessons and had soon reached a standard whereby I could sit at the back of the second violins and saw away in time with the music without causing nausea or brain injury to those sitting around me.

It was there that I witnessed conducting for the first time, and quickly came to two conclusions:

1. This was what I wanted to do.

2. I did not want to do it like that.

Mr. Branston was a kind man, administratively able and loved by the boys for his gentle manner and unremitting enthusiasm for music. On the podium, however, he didn't shine. Even though I had learned everything I knew about music from records, books and Miss Lovejoy, and had therefore never seen a conductor in action, I knew instinctively that whatever conducting was, this wasn't it.

Mild-mannered to a fault in real life, when conducting Branston was transformed by nerves into an ill-tempered martinet. Orchestra rehearsals, which took place on Sunday mornings after chapel, were notably tense affairs, as we took on pieces quite beyond our capabilities to the accompaniment of arrhythmic flounderings and desperate exhortations from the front.

His manual technique was, if one is being generous, rudimentary, and hindered by the fact that his head was buried in the score. He raised the music stand up to chin level so that he could see the music, and his asynchronous arms waved in our general direction from either side of it. Occasionally he would look up in surprise and hurl a cue at an instrument that was already playing. This was almost inevitably followed, shortly after, by an agitated rapping on the music stand or even a stamping of the foot.

'No no no no no! We must get faster here! Please watch the beat!' he admonished the air in his immediate vicinity, and then he was off again, flailing to and fro in the vain hope that the sound would somehow appear and match itself to his incomprehensible wagglings.

Thus he worked his way through the orchestral repertoire, murdering one piece after another in an anti-musical orgy of genocidal proportions. No composer was immune, and sometimes it seemed as if the orchestra were merely collateral damage.

What was most frustrating was that we knew he didn't do it deliberately. We shared his desire to get it right, but the signals he gave us were so disturbing to the music that nobody stood a chance. Any efforts to communicate amongst ourselves contradicted what he did, and his conducting style was so active that it was impossible to ignore him.

Furthermore, his own musicality was getting in the way. When he heard something wrong it put him off his stroke, his gestures became more uncertain, leading in turn to more mistakes from the orchestra, and so on. It was a self-perpetuating cycle of cause and effect from which there could emerge no winners, merely battered and exhausted participants whose will to live had been through the mangle so often that it could now only utter a feeble mewing sound from its position in the cold, dark trough of bleak reality.

It would have been better, in a way, if he had been blissfully unaware of the sounds made by the orchestra. Then he would merely have waved his arms in time to the sounds in his head and allowed the players to ignore him.

Things didn't get better when he stopped to rehearse. His painstaking attempts at clarity only served to obfuscate and confuse.

'This passage must be executed in such a manner as to seize the...um...audience, the listener, with a sense of the strength that the passage conveys, a rhythmic strength, and not just a rhythmic one, but a strong sense of...strength...in...the...errm...execution...it must be very...strong. Violins...no, I mean violas...and of course cellos...all the strings...you must play the rhythm with...strength...'

'Woodwinds—please, in bar 66, after the first quaver, that is except the bassoons who have a crotchet there, on the first beat, but after that, for everyone else, the remaining quavers until the fourth beat, where the clarinets have semiquavers, which have to be staccato and very clearly...staccato...the quavers, the legato ones in the oboes and flutes, but not the crotchet in the bassoons...please, make sure they are truly legato...but not too much...'

'Brass, where you have *piano* marked, please make it more, not less...*piano*, that is...at the moment it's not enough...*piano*...'

Occasionally he would make ill-advised and disastrous forays into the realms of metaphor.

'Imagine that this passage is a layer of velvet, but with rocks underneath making it stick up in places, and iron filings clinging to the sides, but only some of them, so the others slip to the bottom and gather in a pool...'

'This is like a soaring bird floating towards the sunset, just flapping its wings occasionally, but then some rain clouds appear, so it has to flap its wings more often, and then the sun sets and all around is obscure. Play it like that.'

Even the more experienced players were still in relatively early stages of their development, and lacked the confidence to counteract Branston's malign influence. So even though we gradually got to know our parts better as the rehearsal period wore on, everything he said and did merely confused us more, while his manner of delivery eroded our confidence to the point where we were afraid to do anything lest we incur his wrath.

As I sat disconsolately trying to fit the second violin part of Dvořák's Eighth Symphony into the stuttering mess of gestures being hurled at us from the front, I tried to work out exactly what it was that Branston was doing wrong.

My first answer was simple: everything.

Dismissing this as glib and unhelpful, my better self asked for more information.

'His beat's not clear, he doesn't look at the players and he gets angry with them for the unforgivable sin of acting on his mistakes. How's that for starters?' responded my cynical-before-its-time other half.

'And I suppose you could do better?'

'Damn right.'

The kernel of an idea formed at the back of my mind. Two months later the Emanon Ensemble made its debut.

I had started.

CAST YOUR MIND BACK to your first driving lesson. The vehicle seems to have a mind of its own, the steering wheel and gas pedal have the opposite effect to what is desired, and it is all you can do to keep the unruly brute on the road.

So it was with my first rehearsal as a conductor.

Half an hour into Emanon's existence, I was beginning to have some sympathy with Mr. Branston's weekly plight. Why on earth did the players insist on taking a faster speed than the one I was showing? And why did they then slow down so that I had to vary the speed of my beat to stay with them? And why could the idiots not play together?

Even worse than this was a phenomenon that seemed quite inexplicable to me. When sitting in the orchestra, I kept myself interested in proceedings by making a mental checklist of mistakes I heard in the orchestra around me. Ensemble, rhythm, intonation—all these and more came under my expert scrutiny, and as I ticked them off in my head I noted with growing scorn Mr. Branston's apparent indifference to them. Yet here I was, in his position, and I was unable to make head or tail of what I was hearing.

I had chosen a short programme for chamber orchestra with which to make my debut, and had scheduled it as part of the monthly pupils' concerts that were put on by the music department to give young musicians some experience of performing in public. I was obliged by the terms of my scholarship to participate in two of these each term, and I had pleaded with Mr. Branston to be allowed to use this conducting outing as one of my quota.

As we struggled to settle a simple Mozart march at a speed that wouldn't seem to represent a platoon of soldiers so inebriated that they could barely stand, I made a silent vow never to mock Mr. Branston again.

This was harder than it looked.

I HAVE REPRESSED THE MEMORY of Emanon's first concert for so long that it is as much as I can do to dredge up snippets of detail from it. The absence of the timpanist due to his rustication that morning for possession and use of cannabis; the clarinettist who played on the wrong clarinet, resulting in his being a semitone out from the rest of the orchestra for a whole movement; the trumpeter who came in fortissimo in a movement in which he was not supposed to be playing; the inexorable sliding of a cellist's music from a broken music stand and his vain efforts to stop it; the almost complete collapse of a simple piece of Haydn, the result of some players playing half-speed, some double, and some, completely inexplicably, quadruple...

From this collage one can build a picture of the most disastrous of debuts. I sometimes think I should get credit simply for retaining the drive to perform a second concert in the aftermath of the trauma of the first.

But persevere I did, with marginally less disastrous results. I was, there is no doubt, absolutely atrocious at conducting—honkingly bad. But my incompetence was more than matched by my conviction of my own prowess, to the extent that for the next two years I wallowed in a pool of self-delusion which inhibited progress to a quite alarming degree.

When the breakthrough came, its genesis was from a most unexpected quarter.

## David Branston

IT WAS AN UNFORTUNATE FACT of my life at St. Umbrage's that not nearly enough of it was taken up with music. As well as the dreariness of academic lessons there was the looming presence of sport.

I had nothing against sport *per se*. I was quite happy for it to exist. It was only when it tried to involve me in its tedious exploits that my ears twitched like those of a fawn in the sights of a leopard.

Strange, then, that not only am I now an avid sports fan, but that sport taught me one of the clearest lessons in conducting, and therefore in life. It is one that has been of great use to me over the years—in fact you could say that it has underpinned everything I do, so it is worth exploring in a little detail.

The game of cricket, for those not fortunate enough to know about it, can best be likened, in musical terms, to Wagner's *Ring* cycle: interminable, impenetrable, and, to all outward appearances, a complete waste of everyone's time. Like the *Ring* cycle, it helps if you have been steeped in cricket from an early age; and, also like Wagner's masterpiece, it is surrounded by arcanities and rituals that bewilder even the most curious outsider (and, let's be honest, quite a few insiders as well).

They both also require from the observer great determination and stamina—anyone who has watched Geoffrey Boycott make a century or endured the longueurs of Act Three of *Die Meistersinger* will know what I mean.

But the importance of cricket in my story is more subtle, and has to do with psychology.

At St. Umbrage's I was truly hopeless at the game. Unathletic, and unable to catch, bowl, throw or hit a ball, I managed to avoid playing it for a remarkably long time through a simple ruse designed to enlist the sympathy of my teachers. By the simple expedient of carrying an inhaler about my person, I managed to convince successive teachers and classmates that I was asthmatic, and about to expire without the correct medical intervention. Ah, the power of the inhaler! Never mind that possession of one sent the message that I was a nerdy weakling—that was true enough anyway, and everyone knew it—its true power lay in its ability to render me almost permanently 'off games'.

Then, disaster. I was, as the saying goes, 'grassed up' by a disgruntled contemporary, and my deception was uncovered. I was forced to play, and my cricket career would start in the upcoming Colts 5th XI match against local rivals St. Hubbins' the following Saturday.

I spent the next few days in alternating states of hysteria and paralysis, but somehow managed to make it to the field of play intact.

# David Branston

As we left the pavilion, it occurred to the teacher in charge that he had neglected to name a captain.

'You there!' he called over to me. 'Wossname! You're captain.'

'Who me sir?'

'Yes you sir. Now set your field and look snappy about it!'

'But sir...'

'But sir, but sir...' His voice rose in a mocking impersonation of mine (these were more enlightened times, when to be a teacher meant that you could at any time embarrass or humiliate your charges in a manner of your choosing—indeed, it was expected by both parties). 'But sir, but sir...stop your whining, boy, and get on with it.'

Stifling the familiar pricking behind my eyes, I tried to think clearly. What did cricket captains do? I scoured my brain—my only experience of cricket was from watching it on the television or viewing it from the boundary while my non-asthmatic peers delivered a walloping to one of the markedly inferior schools in the area. In both cases, I realised now, it was quite obvious what captains did: they looked authoritative, seemed to know what they were doing, but in effect did absolutely nothing.

Eureka.

The cricket captain, I saw now, was nothing more than an orchestra conductor in fetching white clothing.

I strode towards the square.

'Foyle, you'll take the bowling from this end. Waterstone, first over from the other end—you'll be better used coming up the hill into the wind, the ball will swing more.' I racked my brains—I had already used up at least 75% of my cricketing jargon, hazily remembered from afternoons listening to Peter West droning on during some interminable John Player League encounter. 'Hatchard—in the covers.'

'On the one?'

'Yes of course,' I snapped.

I had no idea what 'on the one' meant, but some deep-hidden instinct spurred me on. Be decisive, it said. It doesn't matter whether what you say makes any sense—if your tone of voice is convincing, they'll be convinced.

I scanned my teammates—they were assessing me cautiously. This decisiveness was at odds with their experience of me. I tried to ignore them and focus on the task in hand.

'Blackwell and Daunt, you go in the slips. Stanford! Hey, you there! Stanford minor! Deep backward long mid-on!'

Stanford was the one boy in the team even more ineffectual than me. He hesitated, trying to work out the
exact location of my entirely fictitious fielding position.

Fatal error.

'Well, what are you waiting for?'

'Err...where's deep backward...errm whatever you
said?'

I guffawed cruelly.

'Dear oh dear, Stanford. You'd better buck your
ideas up. Off you go!'

Poor Stanford minor. Quite bewildered, he spun on
his heels, and, narrowly avoiding tripping over his own
ankles, headed off into the deep outfield, possibly never
to be seen again.

I turned to the rest of the team. I nearly had them.

'Well come on chaps,' I urged, clapping my hands.
'You all know what to do!'

There was a moment's silence. Then, as if by magic,
my colleagues assembled themselves in more or less
coherent positions just as the opposing batsmen
reached the crease.

'Come on then lads!' I called, making sure the
batsmen heard. 'Remember how we beat Heathdale!
Same drill, you get me?'

Appallingly obvious, of course. But we won the
game at a canter, dismissing the opposition for 36. Our

opening batsmen knocked off the runs in four overs. I didn't touch the ball once.

It was on that day that I learned the most important lesson in my early conducting years. And it gave me the subtitle of this book (now sadly omitted for want of space on the cover): The Art of Doing Nothing At All While Convincing People That You Are Doing Everything.

Unwieldy? Maybe. True? Indubitably.

# [5]

# *Etwas Ruhiger*

THE DAY OF MY father's funeral dawned cold and windy. No use expecting Northamptonshire to change its spots, not even for one of its most loyal sons.

There were fifteen of us in the church that day. More would have been surprising; fewer embarrassing.

Poor Mr. Archbold. Called upon to play Mozart's *Ave Verum Corpus* as the coffin entered, he wilted under the pressure, supplying a rendition that would have been more accurate if a cat had walked up and down the keyboard. I looked over my shoulder at the pew from which my father had, over the years, murdered dozens of hymns, and, quelling a rising urge to pounce on Mr. Archbold and leave him bound and gagged in the west aisle, found myself wanting to giggle.

What better tribute could there possibly be to a man whose life involved no more than a fleeting acquaintance with music than a performance of Mozart that involved no more than a fleeting acquaintance with the notes?

And then I saw the pallbearers enter the church, and the tears came.

M Y FATHER'S SUDDEN DEATH, coming as it did on the same day as my final performance at St. Umbrage's, was in a peculiar way very well timed.

He would never know that it was during this performance, as I conducted the school orchestra and choir in a reasonably convincing rendition of Mozart's *Requiem* (oh the bittersweet irony!), that my decision to become a professional conductor was cemented.

With my school days nearly over, and a year till I would take up my place at Cambridge to read Music, I had been confronted with the dilemma of what to do next.

The burgeoning fashion of the time was to indulge in a 'gap year'.

Perhaps I should travel to South America or Africa to help with one of the thriving charity projects there? Or maybe six months on a ranch in New Zealand? One of my friends was going to the Seychelles to carry out a study of the Aldabra Giant Tortoise.

I had other plans.

I had heard from one of my fellow St. Umbrage inmates of the great conducting pedagogue Professor Etwas Ruhiger.

Professor Ruhiger's performing career had stopped fifteen years earlier, the circumstances shrouded in mystery. Rumours abounded, some outlandish, some unrealistically convoluted, some frankly scary. It is not my place to add fuel to the now barely glowing embers of what at the time seemed like a deliciously horrific scandal. All I will say is that, to my certain knowledge, Professor Ruhiger never admitted a Belgian to his class. Infer from that what you will.

Since ceasing professional conducting activities he had devoted his life to his teaching practice in the beautiful resort of Bütter-am-Wein, helped by his unswerving and seemingly ageless assistant Dieter. Renowned for his rigour, temper, and comically bad English, Professor Ruhiger was the *ne plus ultra* of conducting pedagogues, and it was notoriously difficult to gain admission to his class.

I had applied for the course more in hope than expectation, and had been delighted to receive my acceptance (in nearly impenetrable bureaucratic German) that very morning. The thrill of conducting one of the great works, and of feeling that my contribution to the performance was more help than hindrance, compounded these feelings of ecstasy.

Vague intentions of pursuing music to its logical conclusion, whether or not this would lead to a career, coalesced into one single, burning desire. I could no longer ignore the signs: I would be a conductor. Perhaps, given time, experience and luck, one of the great ones.

Thus, as my father passed from one world to the next, so did I.

S OME WEEKS LATER I presented myself at the front door of Professor Ruhiger's beautiful, sprawling Schloß in the remote region of Germany known locally as the Obendrunterzwischendurch.

The professor's house and grounds occupied several acres on the edge of the Wein lake, in the shadow of the Bütter mountain, whose imposing mass dominated the landscape. All the students (about twenty-five of us) lived on campus, as it were, in one of the many outbuildings that were dotted around the property. There was ample space in the wooded grounds to find the solitude necessary for serious study, and I felt at home at once.

## Etwas Ruhiger

The schedule was rigorous, starting with an hour of yoga at 6am. After breakfast (prunes and yoghurt in the Grimmsaal), the class would assemble in the professor's teaching room. It was Dieter's job to ensure that everything was in order, to take the register, and to check that nobody in the room bore a trace of the many allergens that would hinder the professor's ability to teach, speak, or even breathe.

This duty dispatched, Dieter would fetch Professor Ruhiger while we sat in silent and nervous anticipation. After a few minutes the professor would enter, walking at his usual slow pace. Although he was by no means a frail man, his solid physique forming an imposing presence in the room, he suffered from an unnamed condition that meant he walked very slowly; and yet he was an active sportsman until the very end of his life, and was often to be seen on the tennis court giving Dieter a thorough spanking.

The professor's routine at the beginning of class was invariable. He would greet each student in person, working his way through the class at his own leisurely pace. Professor Ruhiger's master stroke, when executing this process, was not just to address each student by name, but to get every single name wrong. I never once heard him get one right. In order to do this, of course, he had to know everyone's actual name, so as to avoid an embarrassing accident whereby he might by some miracle stumble upon their correct appellation.

This ritual concluded, he would ascend his throne (literally—it had belonged to Landgrave Balthasar of Thuringia), and, with a curt 'Zo, ve begin', he would open the day's formal proceedings.

The main morning session would consist of one of the more experienced students conducting a phrase (sometimes, if they were particularly favoured, two phrases) from one of the dozen or so pieces in the professor's repertoire. The class was conducted in silence, the presence of pianists or orchestra being detrimental, so the professor explained, to the true process of conducting, at least at this formative stage of our development. As the student conducted, we were to hear the phrase in our heads, any discrepancy from the written text being laid firmly at the feet of the errant pupil. A failure to pay due attention to the second flute part, for example, would be clearly discernible by a lack of movement in the little finger of the left hand. Having observed the student's paltry efforts, the professor dissected their every move for the benefit of both pupil and class.

'No! Not zo! Do it uddervize!' he would exhort if, for example, the student had her elbow at the wrong angle to denote a true *pianissimo*. Or, another favourite, 'Ziss iss not legaaaato. Like ZISS ze legaaaato ve are showink!', accompanied by a flawless execution of the gesture in question.

The level of detail was astonishing. I remember one week in which we got no further than the first chord of Beethoven's Seventh Symphony. On another occasion, an increasingly uncomfortable student stood for ninety minutes while the professor adjusted her starting posture, Dieter being the unfortunate executor of his instructions. I well remember the pained expression on poor Dieter's face as he tried to carry out the professor's commands. 'No! Ze boottock iss too metch now leftvarts!' cried the professor, and Dieter muttered an embarrassed apology as he tried to manipulate the poor student's gluteus maximus into a position that was acceptable to the Maestro.

Professor Ruhiger's teaching style was often economical—a favourite exhortation, admirable in its clarity and strength of feeling, was 'Feeple! Vunce more!'—but he was also capable of talking at great length, his every word nonetheless imbued with astonishing depth of meaning, such that we would emerge from the class into the sizzling Bütter sunshine reeling from the intensity of the learning experience. Legend had it that he had devoted a whole day to a single held note in a Mahler symphony.

'Zis G iss mayjic cryestal hengink in ze air. Ven ze condector cut it down, it smesh to ze grount unt shetter!'

He talked of philosophy, the inner meaning of music, its effect on the human psyche, the hidden sexual significance behind the notes, and many other aspects of the music besides. At times he would seem to stray far from the subject, into realms apparently entirely dissociated with the music in question. And then, like a great symphonist, he would draw all the arguments together in a triumphant analysis of why the pupil's wrist was too slack to elicit a proper staccato from the third horn.

If sometimes he was a little far-fetched ('Iss not chust E flet chord—iss towerink mesculine errrrection!' he once roared at a bewildered female student), more often he shed light on the music and the craft of conducting in ways that I have encountered neither before nor since. And on the rare occasions when he stood up to demonstrate his meaning to the class, it was as if the gods themselves had descended into the room to illuminate the music for us. Nobody who was present when he interrupted a pupil's lesson on Rossini's *Silken Ladder Overture* to conduct (in reverent silence, remember) the entirety of Wagner's *Götterdämmerung* will ever forget either the translucence of his interpretation or the deep hunger that began to gnaw at the stomach somewhere around the beginning of Act Two.

Both in class and out of it, there was a strictly defined, but never elucidated, code for addressing him: new students were obliged to use the most formal nomenclature, 'Sehr geehrter Herr Doktor Professor Ruhiger'; after three months in the class, you were allowed to drop either the 'Doktor' or the 'Ruhiger', but not both; after six, the 'Herr' was dispensed with. And so on.

Only one person ever called him 'Etwas'. He wasn't seen again.

To accommodate the cosmopolitan nature of the class, the professor worked in English, a language with which he seemed perennially uncomfortable, and which he spoke with the heaviest of accents. This, we thought, was only to be expected—we assumed, partly because of our location, and partly because of the whole 'Sehr geehrter Herr Doktor Professor' business, as well as the nature of his name itself, that his heritage was Germanic. It emerged, however, that he spoke all languages with a heavy accent—German like an Englishman, French like an Italian, and so on. To this day nobody quite knows what his provenance or mother tongue was, although there was a vicious (and, as always, completely unsubstantiated) rumour circulating that he was the son of Esperanto-speaking Welsh miners and changed his name at the age of twelve from Eddie Llewellyn. The 'Ruhiger' part was supposedly the closest Germanic approximation he could think of to Wales's national sport.

The language barrier, inevitably, led to some mis-understandings. Once, in a lesson devoted to the tempestuous journey that is Tchaikovsky's *Romeo and Juliet Overture*, the professor was trying to give guidance to Gretha, an earnest and timid Swiss pupil whose feeble efforts to conduct music of a passionate and extrovert nature continually left him almost speechless with frustration.

On this occasion he became exasperated by Gretha's inability to master the sword fight passage, with its running semiquavers in the strings and irregular rhythm in the rest of the orchestra.

Gretha, for her part, was exasperated by Professor Ruhiger's inability to master the English language.

'Here iss most important ze condector viz less to ze gesture movement to make.'

Gretha, picking the bones out of the mess of advice contained in the sentence, took a view, and started conducting again with smaller gestures.

The professor wriggled in his seat.

'But for vot like ziss you are condectink? Still metch less! Metch metch less!'

Shaking slightly, the poor girl tried to comply with his wishes, reducing the size of her beat to Lilliputian proportions.

'Nooo!' roared the professor, stamping his 'bad' foot on the ground. 'I say less unt you condect vit more small ze gestures!'

There was a silence. Realisation hung in the air like a bauble from a Christmas tree. Dieter, who from his seat next to the professor had been trying to quell the inexorably growing wrath of the great man, cleared his throat.

'Er, Herr Professor...'

'Vot?' snapped the professor, turning to his trusty aide with fire in his eyes.

Dieter hesitated, a tiddlywink in the path of a tsunami. Yet gamely he carried on.

'I think...there may be a misunderstanding...'

'How? Vot messinderstentment?'

'Is it not possible, Sehr geehrter Herr Doktor Professor, that when you are saying 'less', you are in fact meaning...' he swallowed, dangerously committed, '...more...?'

There followed a silence of whose intensity and duration John Cage would thoroughly have approved.

Then the professor roared with laughter and clapped Dieter on the shoulder, sending him sprawling into the front row of students.

'Yayss!! Yayss!! Iss true!' He turned to Gretha. 'My dear, pliss forgive me, for my English vich zo rodden iss! Condect more! Metch metch more!' And addressing the class, he concluded, 'Zo, ve are finish, yes?'

So saying, he took Gretha by the elbow and steered her out of the room ahead of him.

WHEN I THINK OF THOSE DAYS, I remember many things: the intensity of the learning experience under Professor Ruhiger's inspirational tutelage; the long evenings of solitary study as I tried to root out the inner meaning of the set piece for the next day; the vigorous discussions with my fellow students as we debated the rôle of the third finger in the coaxing of vibrato from the viola section; the importance of a relaxed jaw when conducting music of the Second Viennese School.

The atmosphere in the class was mostly supportive, although the inevitable undercurrent of competitiveness occasionally surged to the surface. This was not something that the professor encouraged. The true worth of our studies was to find a deeper knowledge of the music and therefore ourselves, and not to try to best each other in our search for the 'perfect upbeat' or other such irrelevances.

He was certainly not concerned with the idea of 'career'. For him this was something incidental and not to be valued—he had, to all intents and purposes, abandoned his own performing career at an early age to focus on his calling as a pedagogue. And thereafter he devoted all his energies to the nurturing of his charges. We soon learned that everything he did was for us and us alone, and that what might at the time seem insignificant was always related to our conducting. He once broke wind noisily while a young Greek conductor was attempting to portray the opening phrase of the *Tristan und Isolde Prelude*. Even serious-minded young musicians have their frivolous side, and some of us were unable to contain our giggles, much to the professor's disdain.

Afterwards, Dieter was sent to admonish us.

'It wasn't an accident. It was a comment on Stelios's conducting.'

A few days later, the professor fell asleep while a particularly dour-faced Russian called Dmitri was conducting the first movement of Tchaikovsky's *Manfred*—the only piece I ever saw him conduct, and one that the professor loathed with the burning intensity of a thousand suns. The message of the professor's easy somnolence was not lost on us—Dmitri's conducting was simply not worth staying awake for.

This devotion manifested itself in matters off the podium too, for Ruhiger was a master of what he called The Inner Art. The theory was that conducting is a holistic activity, and therefore its teaching must encompass the whole person. As a result, while we were Professor Ruhiger's guests at Bütter-am-Wein, everything was rigorously micro-managed.

'Ven you of yourself in control are beink, zen only vill you of ze orchestra haff control,' he said on many occasions, the word order changing according to his mood.

At the time I was dismissive of what I regarded as matters of little importance such as clothing and diet. After all, what effect on my conducting could my daily intake of protein possibly have?

It was only during a catastrophic lesson on Mahler's massive Ninth Symphony, following an ill-considered wurst and pretzel binge the night before, that I discovered the answer. My faculties, denuded by the lack of vitamins and proper nourishment, were simply not at the required level for such music. I was weakened to such an extent that the effort of conducting the opening pages left me weak and whimpering. My condition was further enfeebled by the professor's unyielding response to my pathetic efforts. He chewed me up and spat me back out again, his withering scorn plain in every mispronounced syllable.

'Ziss vill not pess. Jest look. From shoelacings epvorts all ze vay to ze tousling of ze hair you vill never, I say NEVER, ziss music be condectink! Vot impudent you are beink! Who ever dit condectink Mahler varing chins?!'

I was in such a state of shock that I could barely understand what the professor was saying. It was only when I saw Dieter looking meaningfully at the lower half of my body that I understood what was going on. Dieter's scrutiny was not in itself an unusual event—indeed even I, stoutly heterosexual as I was, occasionally felt a frisson under his unflinching Teutonic gaze—but there was something about it that made me replay the professor's words in my head.

Chins.

Not chins.

Jeans.

And grubby trainers with frayed laces.

I saw all.

It is simply not possible to conduct Mahler wearing jeans.

Bernstein, maybe. Adams, for sure.

But Mahler? Never.

It's not an exaggeration to say that this was the moment when I truly understood the holistic nature of conducting.

I haven't looked back since.

## Waving, Not Drowning

ALAS, ALL GOOD THINGS come to an end.

Eight years after my unforgettable immersive experience on the Wein, I heard the sad news of Professor Ruhiger's passing. Like many former pupils I was shocked—he had seemed simply indestructible.

Regardless of the possible cost to my now burgeoning career, I cleared my diary for the week and travelled across to Bütter for the funeral, where I met many of my former colleagues. As we commiserated with one another and fondly recalled our great teacher, I reflected on the fact that this was one of the rare occasions when a group of working conductors could be found in the same place.

It was an unrepeatable experience.

I managed to snatch an afternoon on the Wein with Dieter. The Bütter mountain, like the recently deceased professor, loomed large above us, casting its ever-present shadow over our cogitations. Dieter's tousled blond hair caught the sunlight.

'Do you know what the last thing was that the professor said to me?' he asked, his firm sandy-haired arm brushing against mine.

'No.'

'He said 'Dieter, ziss beepink zount, vot iss?' And then he died.'

We walked in silence for a few more minutes. Then I turned to Dieter and hugged him.

'It's how he would have wanted it. Always looking for answers.'

We turned and walked back to the hotel.

I THINK IT SAFE TO SAY that everything I do as a conductor is influenced by Professor Ruhiger. He is my guiding light every moment of every day, and never more so than when I stand before musicians.

True, the connection may not always be apparent. But even when I'm steering a junior clarinet choir through a simplified arrangement of *The Magnificent Seven*, I feel him at my shoulder, urging, coaxing, never losing sight of the music. 'Rrumm! Tumm-da-dumm! Like zo ze rizzim! Iss like etchaculation!'

We shall never see his like again.

# [6]

# Sandy Beeston

THE FIRST YEARS after I left the tender care of Professor Ruhiger were hard.

The ingénu conductor is like an astronaut: opportunities for hands-on experience are rare and potentially disastrous, and people are unlikely to engage you until you have a few successful missions under your belt. There is little you can do about this except persevere and seize every opportunity that arises.

This is all very well in theory, but when opportunities number exactly zero, they're hard to seize.

There was, however, one area that I could control. I had to do something about my name.

A child born with the name Jonathan Busse must become used to the inevitable puns and jokes— 'Busse—stop!' 'Fares please!' and so on. But it was only when I decided that my future lay in conducting that I became aware of the unfortunate and comic incongruity caused by the juxtaposition of my name and my chosen profession. Did I want to spend my life looking at concert posters which read 'Jonathan Busse—conductor'? Surely not.

I therefore resolved to change it. This is, of course, a perfectly normal practice in the performing professions for those who either decide they've had enough of the name bestowed upon them by their parents or who are overtaken by events and forced to do so. It's a little known fact that the famous Hungarian-born conductor Fritz Reiner was for many years known by his given name, Alexander Kappohn. It was only when the time came for his Chicago debut that someone dared mention to him the connotations of that name in that particular city and he changed it to the much less controversial sobriquet by which he became known to a wider audience.

I toyed with several options: Buster Jones, Jonty Antrobus, Jonah ffinch-bbussington, Yonatan Büsser-Staud.

None of them had quite the right feel.

The answer came to me quite suddenly as I was driving to see my mother one autumn day in 1972. Turning off the A603 on the familiar journey to the Cambridgeshire bungalow where she had moved after my father's death, I barely noticed the signpost, such was its familiarity. Then something clicked.

Barrington 3

Orwell 1

And so Barrington Orwell was born, and not a moment too soon.

I immediately felt at home with the name. It had the ring of authenticity. The Britishness of the first name Barrington was neatly offset by the down-to-earth feel of Orwell, and the respective cricketing and literary connotations of the two elements of the name would surely do no harm.

I would be 'Barry' in the profession, of course. The chumminess of the truncation would engender goodwill in my players.

'Who's on today?'

'Barry.'

'Oh yes, good old Barry.'

And, dared I dream...*Sir* Barrington Orwell?

I had to admit that, based on my career thus far, the prospects of such an elevation were slim. I was eking out a living as a peripatetic piano teacher, completely unemployed as a conductor, and increasingly despairing of this situation changing in any way at all.

I attended as many rehearsals of the professional orchestras in London as I could, and there I was lucky to see in action such shining lights as Tchuyaron Legov, Ansty Cowfold and Jonquil 'Fuzzy' Fazackerley. Eager to glean as much information from them as I could, I would approach them after rehearsals and ask for a moment of their time.

Fazackerley, in his kindness, once called me 'young man'. Beyond that, I received little in the way of useful advice or career-advancing help.

The most forthcoming of them all was Sandy Beeston, a genial man of about fifty whose friendliness and transparent honesty had in no way impeded his career. I collared him after a rehearsal at the Royal Festival Hall.

'Advice, eh? How old are you?'

'Twenty-two, sir.'

'Ah well, plenty of time yet. Develop your talent, take every opportunity, however insignificant it may seem, and never back the favourite in the Grand National.'

'Thank you, sir.'

'You might want to change your name, too. Did wonders for me. Got it off a signpost.'

'I've already done that, sir.'

'Oh really? What did you say it was?'

'Barrington Orwell.'

'Oh well. Don't suppose you can change it again. Never mind.'

'It was Jonathan Busse before.'

'Ah, well in that case you're better off. Oh, one more thing. Learn the Franck D minor symphony.'

'Very well, sir. May I ask why?'

'Can't bear the bloody thing. If I'm ever asked to do it, I might ask you to stand in for me.'

And with that, he gave me a friendly pat on the shoulder and sauntered off.

I stood pondering these pearls of wisdom as the orchestra packed up around me. When I looked up, Beeston was by my side again.

'You know what I think the most important thing is? Find your niche. By all means aim for the top, but if you find you like the view halfway up...well...that's good, isn't it?'

And he thrust a piece of paper into my hand.

'Call this chap. He might be able to help you.'

Two months later, I stood in front of an orchestra. They didn't pretend to be great—in truth, even 'good' was an aspiration too far—but neither did I. For me the most important thing was that they paid me, a pleasing practice they have maintained to this day.

As I looked round the room I took in the faces that were turned towards me expectantly, and prepared to address them. It wasn't an ideal view, on the face of it—a mixed-ability group rehearsing in a cold church hall in North London.

But it looked fine to me.

'Ladies and gentlemen, we start with the Franck.'

# *Summary*

ALTHOUGH I HAVE focused on the figures who loomed largest in my personal and musical development, there have inevitably been some omissions. In fact, almost every musician I have had contact with has affected me in some way, however slight.

An oboist coming up with an entirely original phrasing; a percussionist testing the extremes of dynamics; a ten-year-old violinist playing a scale in a way that makes you think 'I don't believe I've ever heard anything like that before.' They've all played their part, and are a constant reminder that you never stop learning.

But if there have been myriad influences, there is no escaping the conclusion that I am what I am because of myself, and nobody else.

These influences helped me keep my bearings in those early years, and nourish my music-making still. And if thirty or more years spent employed in the music world have taught me anything, it is that nothing ever turns out exactly the way you expect it.

Do I wish that I had become the conductor I envisaged all those years ago, touring the concert halls of the world with the great orchestras, darling of the media and the record labels, my name emblazoned on posters from Adelaide to Zurich?

Sometimes.

And do I resent the musicians with whom I work on a daily basis, each one honestly giving of their best to realise the lofty musical ideals towards which we must all constantly strive, no matter how misguided they may be, for the fact that I didn't?

Never.

But enough of this. We must move on to the main course, the reason why you have either soldiered gamely through the first part of the book or have skipped directly to this page.

Conducting.

What's it all about?

# PART TWO

# ACTUAL CONDUCTING

# *Introduction*

I'M OFTEN ASKED, 'How do you become a conductor?' It's the unanswerable question. You might as well ask how many bubbles there are in a perfectly chilled glass of Pol Roger White Label 1993.

The truth is that there is no one way. Years of study and utter dedication to the craft may play no more active a part in a conductor's success than having an uncle on the board of one of the major orchestras. And you can dress a monkey in an emerald Armani polo shirt, but it will still need an infinite amount of time and the service of an infinite number of orchestras before it can execute a passable rendition of *Death and Transfiguration*.

But if the secret to great conducting remains intangible, there are still methods available to even the most incompetent charlatan (it would be invidious to mention names) that can enable him to fool most of the people most of the time.

I'm not implying that conductors are engaged in some kind of deception or trickery. Good heavens no!

Well...yes.

81

Many is the mediocre performance that has been transformed in the minds of the audience into a Great Occasion by the demeanour of the conductor. Call it confidence, chutzpah, charisma or what you will— there is Something About Them that makes people sit up and take notice. People in the audience, that is. The orchestra may not have got the memo. They're more concerned with whether the conductor's gestures bear any relation to the music in front of them.

Imbued with this mystical aura, the conductor can pull a fast one on the hapless punters, who in turn play their part by suspending their critical faculties. Unplayable tempi become 'a breathtaking whirlwind'; ragged ensemble is 'taking risks'; a slow movement that loses momentum to the point of stasis has 'a true and old-fashioned sense of breadth', and so on.

Does this matter? In the grand scheme of things, no. Bear in mind that in a couple of billion years all life on Earth will have ceased to exist due to the inexorable rise in temperature of the sun, so the relative merits of two contrasting interpretations of Shostakovich's Eighth Symphony may be rendered somewhat irrelevant. (Remember: it's part of the conductor's job always to see the big picture.)

So what is it that a conductor actually does? And how does one go about it? In the pages that follow, I will attempt a meagre explanation.

# GENERAL ISSUES

# [7]

# *Conductor Types*

B EFORE DEALING with the intricacies of technique, we should take a moment to consider the kind of conductor you want to be. This is not a decision to be taken lightly, after all. Your persona will dictate everything about your conducting, from the size of your upbeat to the softness of your polo shirt.

While it may be true that you can only be yourself, it can do no harm to spend some time in advance pondering exactly which version of 'yourself' you would like to be. Everyone's different, of course, but if you are to present yourself to an unsuspecting public, you need to have an identifiable personality. For this to happen you need a personality—lacking this, you might be better off becoming a politician.

There are many different types of conductor, and the few that follow below are merely archetypes—most people choose one dominant type, with sprinklings from other categories. Think of it as a really delicious curry. When you have the mix right, no single flavour predominates and each ingredient is held in perfect balance with the others, allowing the whole dish to sing; get it wrong, and you'll be the chicken korma of conductors—beige, sludgy, and the choice of those who don't know what they want.

## The Scholar

Slender, delicate-looking, studiedly distrait, with wispy hair flying to and fro in the slightest breeze, this conductor exudes knowledge and thought, if not charisma. Wire-rimmed half-moon spectacles are a must, the implication being that long hours have been spent researching in libraries. He will make much of the minutiae.

'Ah, now then. This staccato marking in the second flute part—the cause of much debate. Some sources have it legato, of course, but their authenticity is dubious...'

That kind of thing.

The Scholar can get so bogged down in these details that rehearsals rarely progress beyond the first movement exposition, and orchestras are left to fend for themselves in the later movements, which are usually much more difficult.

## Conductor Types

### The Jolly Good Chap

The 'hail fellow well met' type: English, exuberant, jovial, openly pally with everyone, he can often be found in the cafe holding forth on one subject or another, punctuating his story-telling with sharp barks of laughter at his own jokes.

But beware. Behind that smile lurk shark's teeth. He has played this part for years, and will probably get rid of half the orchestra the moment he's appointed Music Director.

### The Wild Man of Borneo

'Keep your hands and feet away from the cage' might be an appropriate sign to hang near this conductor. Exuding animal power, he (and it's always a he) seems to prowl the podium like a caged panther. While conducting he emits bestial grunts, and front desk players may need masks to protect against flying drool. His conducting style comes under the heading 'rampage'. Adrenal prestissimi are as likely as excessively drawn out adagios. Once in a while this will result in a performance so electrifying that it will all, momentarily at least, seem to be worth it. Critics will hail The Wild Man a genius, driving him to yet further extremes and orchestral musicians to drink.

### The Out-And-Out Bastard
At least you know where you stand. He's a shit, and doesn't mind who knows it. It doesn't matter where you're standing—he will manage to stab you in the back anyway. You might as well take your punishment, chalk it up to experience, and moan about him along with everyone else.

### The Lazy Bugger
He has a tendency to, shall we say, not push rehearsal times to their limits. Possibly the greatest example (and, incidentally, a quite majestic conductor on his all-too-rare day) was Horace Ontahl. Engaged by a big London orchestra to conduct a programme including Stravinsky's *Rite of Spring*, he played no more than three minutes of the opening, laid down his baton and asked:

'Ladies and gentlemen, you appear to know the piece very well. When did you last play it?'

'About six months ago, Maestro.'

'And who was conducting?'

Upon being told the name of a meticulous colleague and rival, he slapped shut the score and said: 'Oh he's *very* good. You'll be fine. See you later.'

In later years he would only accept engagements in towns where there was a restaurant with at least two

Michelin stars, and insisted on a clause in his contract stipulating a maximum of two hours of rehearsal a day.

Renowned English conductor Linby Hucknall, on the other hand, refused to work on days when there was a cricket international being played anywhere in the world, and once scheduled a tour to Australia to coincide with the Ashes series being played at the same time. The resultant lean schedule, with its concomitant *per diem* payments to every single player, effectively bankrupted the orchestra.

## The Cosmopolitan

Smooth, suave, sophisticated, The Cosmopolitan is the most socially acceptable conductor there is. Often to be seen gracing the pages of the glossy magazines, he's on first-name terms with members of royal families in at least six countries, and acted as best man at the weddings of two of them. He has homes in exclusive areas of London, Madrid, New York and Buenos Aires, along with, of course, the requisite mistresses.

An extravagantly talented all-round musician, he plays several instruments to a very high standard. As a conductor, he possesses a flawless technique, consummate aural skills and a photographic memory. He commands exorbitant fees, for sure, but is also a shrewd businessman and delivers packed houses, glowing reviews and stratospheric record sales on a regular and ongoing basis.

Despite all this, he has no friends in the whole world. Not one. This is because he's a complete prick.

## Mr. Particular

He's not picky, he just likes things the way he wants them. In rehearsal, he conducts with a perpetually pained expression, as if even the most transcendent playing just doesn't quite do it. Before he makes a comment, he says 'It's just fine. Really.' Everyone in the room knows not only that he doesn't mean it, but that it's the closest they're going to get to a compliment. In the ensuing rehearsal, he fusses over sight lines and extraneous noises. Then he asks his assistant to investigate a draught 'howling through the hall—like a typhoon' which is perceptible only to him.

He has his batons made for him, to precisely specified length and weight, by 'the most wonderful little man in Ghent. A true craftsman. You can hear the difference it makes to the sound.'

This fussiness extends to his out-of-hours behaviour. When arriving at a hotel in a new city, he asks to see the chef and gives him his mother's recipe for chicken soup, to be served 'piping hot, in a white china bowl, with the crispest linen napkin.' He then organises a series of 'one-on-one' chats with each principal player, during the course of which he induces them to say nasty things about the others—information which he will, naturally, use to his advantage when the time comes.

## The Brooder

Pale of visage, as if he has not seen the light of day in months, The Brooder is intense, humourless, and especially good at Tchaikovsky. He conducts as if he is stirring a huge cauldron of soup, with occasional lurches denoting that he may have speared a chunk of meat. Monosyllabic in rehearsal, he often leaves orchestras in the dark as to what his real intentions are, beyond the very basic fact that they're serious. In concert, he glares at the orchestra as if challenging them to defy him. Rumour has it that he last told a joke in 1983. It wasn't funny, so he forswore them from that day onwards.

## The Grand Old Man

He's been around for ever, and has been taken for granted for nearly as long. But now, having reached the venerable age of eighty or so, he comes into his own. Ignoring the fact that they publicly despised and scorned him for decades, the critics hail him as 'the leading light of the older generation of conductors', 'evoking an era that we thought had disappeared', and 'leaving younger and more lauded colleagues trailing in his wake.'

The truth is, though, that he's conducting exactly as he has always done, just a little slower. He accepts the plaudits (and renewed contracts) with genial good grace until, in the middle of an inexorably decelerating performance of Bruckner's Seventh Symphony, his heart, in sympathy with the music, stops.

You may have to wait a while before being able to pull this one off, but there's no harm in laying the foundations early. The finest exponent of the 'old before his time' feel was surely Jonquil 'Fuzzy' Fazackerley, whose star burned bright, and all too brief, in the seventies.

Fazackerley's real name was John Fisk, but a judicious name change at the age of ten laid the foundations for what many assumed was going to be a long and successful career.

Deliberately at odds with the burgeoning fashion for informality that prevailed at the time, he invariably wore a three-piece suit to rehearsal, eschewed a wristwatch in favour of a half-hunter fob that he kept in his waistcoat pocket, and on occasion sported a monocle which he would allow to dangle against his conductor's desk while he conducted. Rumour had it that he was also a user of snuff.

Fazackerley had a preference for English music from the first part of the century, especially his beloved Elgar, whose œuvre he explored with tedious doggedness. He spoke with the booming, gravelly voice of a man twice his age, and like one who is used to communicating outdoors, perhaps on a hunt. In addition, he appended many of his sentences with exclamations of the kind that had died out forty years earlier.

'Horns, quieter at letter P, hey?' he would boom. Or, 'Will you please ensure that the rhythm is exact, dash it!' Or, 'Steady on, everyone, or we'll all end up in the drink. Yarooks!'

At the end of each rehearsal he would sit for a few minutes on his stool as if exhausted to the point of collapse, and then ask if somebody would be so kind as to pass him his stick, a weathered knobkerry that one wouldn't have been surprised if he had used personally in the Boer War. Before descending from the stool, he would take a small white pill 'for the old ticker', then leave the rehearsal hall, pausing only for a breather by the entrance desk.

When I first witnessed this display he was twenty-eight years old.

For all this ostentatious old-agery, Fazackerley was admired and loved by those with whom he worked, and his tragic death at the age of thirty-five (attributed in some quarters to 'extreme old age') was mourned in one orchestra, without irony, by the wearing of black for three months.

## The Dude

He's relaxed, probably in his mid-thirties, listens to hip-hop and thrash metal, and is as likely to pro-gramme Frank Zappa as Zemlinsky—but probably not Beethoven ('Hey, gotta know your limits'). Prone to saying things like 'Jeez guys, you really blow me away' or (in a Brahms symphony) 'It's the darnedest thing—it's great, but just needs...you know...a bit of Basie, ok?' or 'Has anyone else noticed how much like Radiohead this sounds? There's a sort of...chewiness to it', or (laying down his baton in a gesture of cloyingly false humility) 'I'll do you a deal, folks—play it right and I'll try not to ruin it'.

His pre-concert talks have become an occasion in themselves, and are usually better attended than the concerts that follow them. In them he will engage with the audience in a way that will make the idle observer recall Macbeth: 'A tale told by an idiot, full of sound and fury, signifying nothing.'

The punters love it though. Nobody ever accused The Dude of being a deep thinker, but he's great box office.

**The Ears**

Hears EVERYTHING. Third desk violas beware—this conductor will notice when you're an eighth of a tone sharp or the proverbial gnat's crotchet ahead. But don't be afraid—while his ear for detail is awe-inspiring, it's only matched by his inability to hold a tempo or conduct a pause.

# Female Conductors

IT GRIEVES ME THAT I SHOULD NEED to make the distinction between the genders. But, as there are conductor types that are exclusively the preserve of men, so there exist Women Only classes.

There is no denying that, in a reflection of their place in society over centuries, women conductors have greater hurdles to overcome than men. With conducting well established, alongside football managing and chief-executive-ing, as an almost exclusively male domain, any woman wanting to join the club has had to prove herself at least twice over.

Women may be discouraged by this. But don't despair. For you will find that, in a rare display of genuine equality, orchestras are capable of ignoring women on the podium just as much as their male counterparts, and with equal relish.

The relatively recent emergence of women conductors has necessarily meant that archetypes are as yet rare. But here are a few of the most obvious:

The Power Dresser

Shoulder pads may have gone out in the eighties, but nobody has told her. Brutally efficient, scarily bright and magnificently self-assured, she flings her rehearsal points rapidly in all directions like someone scattering seed for pigeons. There's no doubt she covers more ground than many others, and everything is very polished, but there is more than an element of box-ticking about both rehearsals and performances.

The Wafter

She cuts an elegant figure on the podium, swaying this way and that, and with a wan smile trembling on her lips. Willowy to the point of elasticity, she finds herself unable to express anything louder than a *mezzo piano* without getting a terrible pain in her shoulders. Wonderful Mozart, execrable Mahler.

The Pocket Rocket

Short, slim, harmless looking. Don't be fooled. Her energy, once unleashed, is in danger of singeing the eyebrows of anyone careless enough to stand close. She speaks alarmingly quickly in up to six languages, slipping from one to another with practised ease, and her pugnacity reveals itself in a barbed wit that punctures the rampant ego of even the most testosterone-fuelled male.

A ND FINALLY, A CONDUCTOR type for both genders:

## The Perfectly Normal Person
There is no room in the conducting profession for a person like this. Do something else.

# [8]

# *Clothing*

FIRST, A DISCLAIMER. I am a man. Any efforts on my part to dispense wisdom on the subject of female clothing would be risible at best, actively harmful to the human psyche at worst.

I therefore refrain from any such presumption. You, the female conductor, will know far better than I what works best for you.

Try to avoid clunky heels, though. They're unbecoming.

So.

Having established the persona you will wear for the rest of your professional life, you may think you're ready to go, but there are still decisions to be made.

Consider clothing very carefully. In your early days as a conductor you may be financially restricted, and this is bound to inhibit freedom of choice. It's no fun having Hugo Boss tastes on a Primark budget, but this needn't be a hindrance. Indeed, if your clothing outstrips your reputation and experience you risk being labelled as having ideas above your station. It's no use dressing as a Grand Old Man when you look like Justin Bieber.

Consider how best to match your clothing to your persona. The Wild Man of Borneo look will not be enhanced by Boden. Similarly, if you're aiming to cast yourself as a cosmopolitan man-about-town, you can't just kit yourself out at your local UNIQLO.

You may infer, from the emphasis I place on clothing, and the frequent mentions it gets in this book, that I advise you to be expensively and immaculately dressed at all times. Nothing could be further from the truth. The key thing is this: let the clothing match the persona. Consistency is paramount. If you sport a Gieves & Hawkes cashmere jersey with grey flannel trousers and Bruno Magli moccasins one day, don't expect anyone to respect you if you 'rock up' wearing lime-green jeans and Converse All Stars the next. The message of the one will be completely undermined by the other.

And if you really are impoverished, consider the option of buying in bulk. A simple look of a dark-coloured polo shirt with khaki chinos may be hackneyed, but if enhanced with an effective hairstyle it can serve your purpose most efficiently, although you run the risk of anonymity unless your conducting style is extravagantly memorable (for better or for worse). Simple but effective accessories can be useful here: a plain but stylish watch, maybe a brightly coloured handkerchief, at a pinch a bracelet or necklace. All of these tell their own story.

Perhaps the most audacious use of accessories I have ever seen was the narrow black armband worn by erstwhile doyen of the podium Ansty Cowfold, in honour, so it appeared, of his recently deceased mother. His tactic was most subtle. Rather than flaunt his grief, he would keep the armband in his baton case, only putting it on after rehearsal was finished and all the players were packing up. He was, however, careful to make sure that at least one member of the orchestra saw him putting it on. If asked about it, he merely shook his head quickly and stifled the smallest of sobs before scurrying off to his dressing room. The next day he would be found at the podium five minutes before rehearsal, reading from a worn piece of paper, which he would then drop as he tried to put it into his pocket. The helpful player who picked it up for him would see the words 'from your ever-loving mother' written at the bottom of the sheet. Thanking the player, Cowfold would say something on the lines of 'Ah well, nothing to be done. That was last week and this...well, life continues...'

As a sympathy-garnering tactic, it was without peer. Even the most hostile of players would be quelled, and Cowfold could get away with remarkably shoddy conducting under the umbrella of his grief. He could not, of course, deploy the tactic twice in the same place, but managed to get away with it thanks to his wildly peripatetic schedule. He apparently used this 'bravely grieving' tactic everywhere he went for three years before anyone thought to question the veracity of his claim. It turned out, after some surreptitious digging from a player whose brother was a private detective, that his mother was alive, healthy and living in Chigwell.

In one of life's supreme ironies, she was run over by a milk float six months later, and Cowfold's genuine grief was not believed. He drifted into obscurity and retired two years later, a broken man.

In my opinion, the sad postscript to the story does not diminish the effectiveness of the original ploy. His mistake was merely to overuse it.

# [9]

# *Accent*

THE VOICE IS a matter of great importance. Pitch, timbre, accent, inflection—all influence the impression you make, whether in interview, rehearsal or even performance.

You may choose to use your own voice. This is understandable. The adoption of an accent takes many hours of hard work in private until absolute security is achieved. And in the first days of public use you'll need your wits about you to avoid your real voice bubbling disastrously to the surface.

Why bother, then?

This is a valid point, and I would never condemn any conductor for using his own voice.

There may be instances, however, in which it is necessary to consider vocal enhancements (or realignment in some cases). Maybe you have a deeply irritating voice in one form or another: whiny, nasal, adenoidal, cracked, monotonous, ludicrously high-pitched or a combination of such factors. All these can adversely affect your influence on an orchestra, in which case it can be advisable to find a good speech coach and get down to it. The hard work will pay off in the end, and it's all tax-deductible (under the heading 'Vocational Training').

So what kind of accent?

Let this proverb be your guide: 'A prophet is not without honour save in his own country.'

Foreigners go down well, so if you're English, be mid-European; if American, be British, and so on.

The accent needn't be broad, but a hint of mittel-Europäisch can help in any situation, if for no other reason than that it conveys the impression that you spend so much time out of the country that you have picked up a slight accent on your travels.

There's no need to hammer it home, though. An occasional change of word order, implying that you have become more accustomed to a German sentence structure, is one thing. An exaggerated hotchpotch of accents and dialects, on the lines of 's'il vous plaît, laydeess unt chentlemen, wir machen es from ze figura settanta tre' is probably too much egg for that particular pudding.

In the hands of a master, a whole career can be based on an accent. The legendary Arturo Toscanini is a perfect example. He was, of course, a truly great conductor. But in his early years, as plain old Arthur Tusk, son of a Lewisham costermonger, he worked harder on his comedy Italian accent and tempestuous personality than he ever did on learning scores. The dividends he reaped from those years of hard toil were, of course, monumental.

Related to the accent issue is the question of languages. It's entirely possible that you will at some time or other work in a country where English is not the first language. Such situations can be a test of any conductor. You can of course get away with a certain amount by miming and singing, the two universal languages guaranteed to be understood by any orchestra. But when you want to express yourself more deeply you may have to resort to localese, a few words of which you will no doubt have picked up from a phrase book bought at the airport and studied on the plane.

If feeling particularly stubborn, you can of course just plough on in English. If this is your chosen path, try to be as idiosyncratic as possible, using unnecessarily long words, impenetrable sentence constructions, and even completely made-up vocabulary. Even those orchestra members who speak good English will be flummoxed. For example, don't say 'Please, the chord must be very strong at letter C, with great depth of sound.' Rather something like this: 'My most esteemed colleagues, in order to effect the innermost meaning of this passage, we must, by preference, infuse the aggregation of sounds with a profundity of resonance.'

If an advanced linguist, you should be able to speak a smattering of languages, as appropriate, but *always with an intangible accent of some kind.* So, for example, if in Russia, your Russian should be clearly not good enough to convince Russians that you're one of them, but should leave them wondering whether you're English, American or French.

# [10]

# *Demeanour*

IT'S GENERALLY ASSUMED by the layperson that the conductor is a strutting, swaggering, self-assured cock-of-the-walk type, raven locks laden with gel, and his entire being oozing power, sex appeal and a smouldering charisma.

Nothing could be further from the truth—for one thing, hair gel is completely out of fashion nowadays.

As we've seen in the preceding chapters, there are many ways to skin this particular cat, with people of all personality types becoming successful (and even on occasion competent) conductors. Charisma takes many forms, after all, and sometimes people are impressed by characteristics that defy prediction or analysis.

But is there a common thread uniting them all, an ideal for which the eager student can aim?

Possibly.

Talk to musicians about their favourite conductors (often a short conversation) and you will in all likelihood hear the word 'humility' more often than anything else.

'He had exceptional humility—his goal was always to serve the music.'

It may seem then that this is the way to go—show that you're serving the music and you'll be in the clear, regardless of any unattractive personal traits you may display.

Easier said than done. It's no use just pretending to serve the music. False humility may be easy to adopt, but more often than not it's as obvious as a cat in a bowl of satsumas, and manifests itself in a nausea-inducing display of cloyingness likely to win first prize in a Uriah Heep impersonation competition. Unless you can really pull it off convincingly, you'd be better off being true to your own inner arrogance and inflated sense of self-worth. The shy Führer is a rare beast indeed, and musicians and audiences alike prefer a blatant egotist of genuine brilliance to a charlatan in a hairshirt.

# TECHNICAL ASPECTS

# [11]

# *Basic Principles*

W HAT IS 'TECHNIQUE'? Is it merely clarity of gesture? If so, what is clarity?

And so the long day wears on.

Technique, for want of a better word, comprises many aspects, some of which are explored in this section. You may be surprised by some omissions—there's no mention of 'The Left Hand', for example. Nor do I address the thorny issues of music-stand height or page-turning techniques. And the section on Beating Patterns is deliberately cursory. For those obsessed with such arcanities, there are many other texts available that deal with them in dense, soporific detail.

No, I aim to deal with the WHOLE CONDUCTOR, and as such have tried to winkle out nuggets of information that may contain kernels of truth that can be applied holistically to this enormous subject.

We start with an all-too-rarely explored area.

# Before You Start

THE TIME HAS COME. You've prepared yourself as well as possible, exploring every aspect of the programme in intricate detail, and executing countless run-throughs in front of the mirror in your room at home. The rehearsal schedule has been planned meticulously, ensuring that appropriate attention is paid to each piece, and enough time is allocated to the rehearsal of problematic passages.

It's time for the first rehearsal.

Brown suede Hilfigers?

Check.

Cerise Ralph Lauren polo shirt?

Check.

Spare cerise Ralph Lauren polo shirt for after the break?

Check.

Hair?

Check-check-checkeroo.

You're ready.

A lot of people think that the conductor's work is done in performance; still more are under the impression that it's in rehearsal that the Maestro makes the difference; yet others will say that it's in the preparation of the score that the kernel of the genius lies.

There's truth in all of these points of view. But never underestimate the amount that can be achieved in a sadly unexplored part of the conductor's life: the time before the rehearsal. That is to say, the time when you're at the rehearsal venue waiting for the rehearsal to begin. For it is in these seconds, minutes, and possibly even hours that the conductor can begin to exert an influence on the musicians in an orchestra, and therefore on the music itself.

There are choices to be made. Do you, for instance, deploy the age-old tactic of 'making them wait'?

Nine fifty-seven, and no sign of the conductor; 10.00, the orchestra tunes; 10.07, still no sign; at last, at 10.19 (sometimes even later, and on rare occasions not until the next day) the conductor enters, in animated conversation with his personal assistant, the implication being that whatever business they've been engaged in has been so pressing that it's worth keeping the orchestra waiting. The dangers of this approach are clear, and it's generally not favoured nowadays. One hears stories, possibly apocryphal, of orchestras playing the same trick on conductors.

If feeling radical, you might choose to enter the rehearsal early. Maybe there are a few players in their positions, having a little look at some of the trickier passages in the day's repertoire. It's important, if choosing this option, to enter the hall with some purpose in mind. It's no use just mooching around for twenty minutes—this will make you look weak and ineffectual. You may even be asked to leave by an officious hall employee.

Much better to spend the time correcting (or appearing to correct) a bowing in the part of the fifth desk of the second violins, half-moon glasses perched on the end of your nose (see also Props).

Extreme options are also available. If you're a pianist, and there is a piano available, you might spend the time ostentatiously playing through the score of another piece altogether—the more complex the better. If asked, you can merely say 'Oslo next week' while (and this is the important bit) *continuing to play*. As with so many of the tactics in this book, the implication should be that you're terribly busy. You don't actually need to be going to Oslo next week. (It should go without saying that if you're actually in Oslo at the time you should choose another, equally impressive-sounding city).

119

If you've opted to portray yourself as the 'Ultra-Cool' type, you will of course delay your entry for as long as possible. But it's vital that you begin the rehearsal on the dot of 10.00. Your persona may be laid back to the point of virtual horizontality, but unless you're aspiring towards the 'Lazy Bugger' (a very risky ploy, and one only to be used, in the author's opinion, by those who are well advanced in years or those who genuinely don't give two hoots about their career or the music), the display must mask genuine efficiency and control.

The greatest exponent of the 'Ultra-Cool' persona I have ever seen was undoubtedly Gaston l'Houche-Poupée, the brilliant French conductor who is almost entirely unknown outside his native town of Couchant in the beautiful Fauteuil region, where he held sway for more than thirty years over one of the many excellent regional orchestras France boasts.

I only happened upon this wonderful and inimitable conductor while on holiday in the region one year. Spying a poster for that evening's concert, I thought I would see if I could observe the general rehearsal that would no doubt be scheduled for the afternoon.

I was in luck. As I took my seat at the back of the auditorium, the orchestra was taking the stage. For some ten minutes they warmed up, chatted, and all the other things orchestras do while waiting for the conductor to arrive, and I was able to take stock. The first thing I noticed was that on the podium, which was rather more raised than usual, stood a battered looking green leather armchair of the kind you might find in a solicitor's waiting room. I wondered how it had come to be there, and when it would be removed and either replaced with a stool, as is normal, or not replaced at all. I also noticed that this unusual presence seemed not to bother anyone in the orchestra—indeed, the chair was clearly meant to be there. A couple of minutes before the rehearsal was due to begin, the leader of the orchestra stood up and made a great show of moving the armchair a few inches closer to the cellos, eliciting much mirth from the rest of the orchestra. The atmosphere in general seemed more suited to a large social gathering, and far removed from the serious ambiance more common in British orchestras.

Then, at exactly thirty seconds to three, and just as I wondering when the rehearsal would begin, a slender unshaven man of about thirty-five, wearing shorts and a Che Guevara T-shirt, emerged through one of the doors at the back of the stage. He was smoking a cigarette, carrying a cup of coffee and had a magazine tucked under one arm. Of the conductor there was no sign. The man worked his way through the orchestra to the front and I realised with shock that this unsuitable looking character *was* the conductor. Even more surprisingly, before he reached the podium, he waved his cigarette airily in the general direction of nobody in particular and the orchestra, seamlessly shifting modes from 'party' to 'work', and playing with admirable precision and sensitivity, struck up the opening bars of Beethoven's Fourth Symphony. Once the piece was under way, he shuffled up on to the podium, took his seat in the armchair, and began to read the magazine, keeping time with his cigarette, and taking an occasional sip from his coffee.

There were several astonishing things about this display. On the face of it, Maestro l'Houche-Poupée , as I later discovered he was called, was guilty of the most barbaric unprofessionalism I had ever witnessed. But the orchestra seemed unperturbed, and, more to the point, played absolutely exquisitely for this unlikely character, responding to him as if the turning of a page of the magazine or the taking of a sip of coffee were a finely-honed gesture representing unimaginably profound musical insight.

And maybe they were. Because when it came to the moment in proceedings when he had to stop and actually do some rehearsing, he worked with great efficiency and detail, cataloguing all the ways in which the orchestra's playing had not met expectations, how balance could be improved, rhythm tightened, and so on, all from the depths of the undeniably comfortable looking armchair. And while he did this, the orchestra listened attentively and acted on his requests with quiet respect.

When the rehearsal ended, l'Houche-Poupée stood briskly to his feet, shook the hand of the leader, kissed the principal viola on both cheeks, and with a cheery 'À bientôt!' was gone.

The concert that evening was sensationally good, even though I was disappointed to see that the green armchair no longer graced the stage.

I fully expected l'Houche-Poupée to forge an enviable international career, but he never left Couchant. Perhaps the world wasn't ready for his unorthodox rehearsal methods; or perhaps he couldn't bring himself to relinquish the comfort of the armchair and lacked the confidence to demand it travel with him come what may. Perhaps the armchair demanded too high a salary. Who knows? The workings of the international music scene remain a mystery to the uninitiated. He nonetheless provides an excellent example of what can be achieved with audacious pre-rehearsal technique.

Contrast this with the work of Salazar dos Cervezas, the tempestuous Venezuelan conductor who, in his brief tenure with a major London orchestra, earned the nickname 'the Bermuda triangle'.

Cervezas's pre-rehearsal style was one of exaggerated jocularity and fraternisation. Already ensconced on the stage when players started arriving for a rehearsal, he would engage each one in animated conversation, laughing and joking with them, enquiring after the welfare of their children, swapping restaurant recommendations and so on. An oboist might try to sidle into his seat unnoticed. Cervezas was on him like a flash, sitting on the spare seat next to him with his arm draped relaxedly over the oboist's shoulders, and insisting he tell him how young Theo's football tournament had gone at the weekend. Or his eye might settle on an extra player to whom he had yet to be introduced. Off he would shoot, clasping the player's nervous clammy hand in both of his while maintaining prolonged eye contact and stating over and over what a pleasure it was to have him in the orchestra and he must come to him if he needed anything, no really he must. And his wife's name? Ah how lovely. Children? No? One day soon, maybe. They are truly a blessing. And where did he study? Ah how interesting. Please, any time. His door was open. It would be a pleasure to talk, but now the rehearsal must begin—after all, they couldn't start without the conductor.

And with a jocular laugh and a final squeeze of the hand he would saunter across to the podium, waving at other members of the orchestra as he went.

When rehearsal started, it was as if he had been replaced by his evil twin. The smile disappeared, to be replaced by a dark scowl, and he barked out abrupt orders and admonishments, rounding on whatever poor soul happened to be in his sight line. In fact, regular players soon observed a direct correlation: whoever had been engaged in conversation with him for longest before the rehearsal would be on the receiving end of the fiercest tongue-lashing during it. Word spread, and the orchestra members took to hiding in dressing rooms or lavatories before rehearsals, only emerging to allow the bare minimum time to get on to the stage and ready for a prompt start. Dos Cervezas was now condemned to sit on an empty stage, becoming increasingly bewildered and harassed until a throng of players entered at one minute to ten, all of them cheerfully hailing him but apologetically unable to partake in the delightful conversation they had got used to. Utterly disarmed, he stuttered through rehearsals in a welter of apologies and confusion, achieving little, his authority completely eroded by the orchestra's cunning ploy.

He left the orchestra six months after his appointment, citing 'irreconcilable artistic and working differences.'

Be warned.

# Waving, Not Drowning

IT'S CLEAR FROM THE ABOVE EXAMPLES that bold pre-rehearsal techniques can work wonders or backfire, depending on the inherent charisma and persuasiveness of the conductor in question. L'Houche-Poupée, a naturally easy-going man with great faith in his musicians, saw no need to butter them up, but evolved a working practice that suited both parties equally well without detriment to the finished product. Dos Cervezas, who was by nature an oleaginous and unpleasant individual with no redeeming features whatsoever (and whose death three years ago enables me to write such things about him without fear of reprisal), found that no matter how hard he tried to cover it up, his true nature came to the surface. He might as well have not bothered with the façade and just worked on being an ur-example of The Total Shit.

The young conductor would be well advised to bear all this in mind when formulating a pre-rehearsal technique.

Before leaving the subject of the pre-rehearsal, one further example can be cited, albeit with the important proviso: copy at your peril.

Sir Ampney Cricklade was, of course, a doyen of the conducting scene from the thirties right through to his death in 1978. To observe his pre-rehearsal technique, the result of many years of observation and analysis, was to observe a master at work, and, dare I say it, more enlightening even than watching him conduct.

In his pomp, Cricklade used to arrive at BBC Maida Vale studios at least three hours before the rehearsal. Once in the building, he would not spend this time, as one might expect, sitting in his room engaged in last-minute score preparation. Rather, he sat behind the doorman's desk with his feet up, smoking, eating cashew nuts and engaging the bemused doorman in jovial banter about the previous night's dog meeting at Walthamstow. When the musicians started to arrive, he said to the doorman 'Tell you what, Bert, why don't you have a break? I'll look after things here.' Over the years, he honed this 'only-one-of-the-lads' technique to, and sometimes beyond, its limits. The story goes that he was once found in grubby overalls, cleaning the gentlemen's lavatory floor.

The profoundness and subtlety of this ploy still leave me breathless with admiration.

'It's one thing to be "one of the lads",' he seemed to imply, 'but I am one of *these* lads.' Before the rehearsal had even begun, he had assumed the moral high ground, and no matter what counterploy any of the players used they would come across either as haughty and superior or as merely trying to copy the great man.

THERE IS, IN THE SPORT OF GOLF, a famous axiom: 'You can't win the Open Championship on the first day, but you sure as hell can lose it.'

This applies equally well to conducting, as I hope the above examples illustrate.

With these lessons thoroughly learned and absorbed, you are now ready to consider the possibility of beginning to think about the idea of actually conducting something.

# [13]

# *Standing*

IN ANY ANALYSIS of the conductor's art, there must
be a separation between its different facets, broadly
divisible into the intellectual and the physical. Of
course the two link in many areas, as anyone who has
seen the illuminating DVD 'Pumping Iron & Conducting Wagner's Ring Cycle' can attest. But for our purposes we should keep them distinct.

When analysing the physical aspects of conducting,
we can make this separation quite easily.

### The Body
The body must be still. Not still in an 'I've been told to
be still' kind of way. Just still. There's nothing more
off-putting for the audience than a conductor who
throws himself about like a sapling in a typhoon. If
they wanted to see that, they would be in a plantation
in a typhoon zone rather than a concert hall.

This stillness, like so many of the 'rules' laid down in books such as this, is observed less frequently than one might hope in the great conducting names around the world. A brief examination of international podiums will throw up walkers, jumpers, dancers, and many more besides.

The walker shuffles around the podium on a whim, like a shy dancer at a wedding. His movements are random, although they may occasionally be related to the attractiveness of a second violinist whose eye he wishes to catch. In extreme cases, and where space permits, he will walk off the podium and in front of his music stand to conduct the conclusion of a piece, sometimes knocking the music off the stands of players around him in the process.

The jumper simply can't contain himself. At the moment of greatest excitement he leaps in the air, landing noisily a second or two later, and usually at the time that is most detrimental to both the competence of the performers and the enjoyment of the listeners.

The stamper generally reserves his stamping for moments of great musical bravado. Strauss's *Don Juan* is a favourite piece for the average stamper, as are the more swashbuckling moments in the works of Berlioz. Stamping is also sometimes used at moments of frustration, as if to say to the orchestra, 'Well if you can't see where the downbeat is, listen to this!' In extremis, and absolutely *faute de mieux* (i.e. when the conductor has absolutely no clue how to conduct it) it serves as a gathering point at the beginning of Beethoven's Fifth Symphony.

The **rocker** has no solid base. Rather, he plants one foot in front of the other and keeps up a relentless to and fro motion, like a runner at the start of a 1,500-metre race that never begins. This movement, incidentally, must bear absolutely no relation to the rhythm of the music being played, not even a tangential one. This will render it as unhelpful and distracting to the musicians as is humanly possible, regardless of what genius is being transmitted through the arms.

The **swayer** bends at the hips in an almost impossible way, legs rigid, arms cutting a swathe through the air that threatens the personal safety of unwary front desk string players. This may or may not be accompanied by seemingly unrelated grunting.

Sometimes you will find a conductor who walks, jumps, stamps, rocks, sways and dances all at the same time, in a grotesque parody of St. Vitus Dance, limbs flailing spasmodically in every direction as the benighted orchestra tries to keep track of which part of the body they're supposed to be taking their cue from.

Let yourself be none of these. Let yourself be still.

As a measure of the importance of stillness, it should only suffice to mention that Professor Ruhiger ran an annual three-week summer course on the subject. Marrying the intellectual rigour of the Alexander Technique with the torture tactics of the Gestapo, the course remained highly popular with students until its unfortunate discontinuation at the hands of the local Health and Safety Executive.

Morning sessions focused on relaxation techniques, inducing in the students a feeling of wellbeing that would enable their bodies to relax under the greatest of stress. Afternoon sessions put this work to the test, by the simple expedient of electronic sensors attached to sensitive areas of the body. Should any extraneous movement be detected, a small but nonetheless agonising shock was administered. Monitoring closely the recovery time of the student, Professor Ruhiger tailored the treatment to the individual, allowing each pupil to grow at his own pace. At the start of the course the sensors were set to minimum sensitivity, allowing, as is natural with those not used to such discipline, a certain amount of movement. Over the three weeks the equipment was gradually adjusted and tolerance levels honed, so that by the end of the course even the twitchiest of students was able to stand motionless for almost indefinite periods.

So effective was the treatment that I can always tell a conductor who attended one of these courses by his absolute stillness on the podium as well as the nervous expression on his face.

ONCE YOU HAVE MASTERED this stillness, a question will likely pop into your head.

What next?

What indeed?

If the body must be still, it is axiomatic that the arms shouldn't be, otherwise you will have difficulty controlling the music, or even starting it at all (but see Gnothi Seauton in Chapter 15).

### The Arms

The arms are, in many ways, the most important part of a conductor's armoury. They are, after all, the bits that move the most. The problems associated with them, however, are fewer than you might think, and can be itemised quite simply and briefly:

Upper arms pinned to the sides—you conduct as if trying to escape from a straitjacket.

Upper arms too high—you conduct as if trying to attract someone's attention in a crowd.

Upper arms too low—how do you expect them to see what you're doing?

Arms too extended—you resemble an extra from Michael Jackson's 'Thriller' video.

Arms too floppy—you resemble a Thunderbird (also known as the 'Furtwängler').

Elbows too mobile—chicken impersonation.

Elbows too stiff—your arms start to hurt so much after three minutes of conducting that you want to chop them off.

And that's about it. These problems can be addressed and corrected quite simply.

Sadly this cannot be said of the next problem area.


The Face

*'In ze fess iss ze holl vurlt'—Professor Etwas Ruhiger.*

How much truth there is in those seven words, however you choose to pronounce them.

Imagine a conductor with the most expressive hands you have ever seen, capable of showing the elegance of a phrase in exquisite simplicity while at the same time moulding the sound of an entire orchestra. This is indeed a worthy ideal for which to aim, but it's worthless if all anyone can focus on is a face seemingly chiselled from granite, exuding no emotion or human warmth whatsoever, and conveying merely boredom.

By the same token, no amount of histrionic gurning will make up for a total lack of manual technique.

Balance, as always, is the key. If your facial expressions induce hysteria or vomiting, perhaps you've gone too far; if your orchestra play as if in a coma, perhaps they're merely reflecting a vital lack of animation in your face.

Solving the problems of the face can be a troublesome process. The moment a student conductor is made aware of an imperfection, he tends to focus on overcoming it. The level of concentration required to do this, however, can induce a rictus-like expression, as if he is straining to...well, delicacy forbids.

Some rules of thumb:

1. Try to reflect the character of the music. A cheeky wink and a smile can soothe nerves and engender a feeling of camaraderie, but perhaps the last movement of *Das Lied von der Erde* isn't the moment to unveil them. By the same token, Leroy Anderson's music rarely benefits from a conductor whose facial expression would be more appropriate to someone who has just lost a much-loved relative.

2. There is a fine line between eye contact and sexual harassment.

3. No matter how moved you are by your own genius, never cry.

# [14]

# *Starting*

L ET'S IMAGINE that you are standing in front of an orchestra, about to begin a piece. Let's also imagine, for the sake of simplicity, that this piece begins on the first beat of the bar[1].

---

[1] There are occasions when the composer, in wilful defiance of the conductor's wishes, starts a piece with a single instrument (the most famous examples are Stravinsky's *Rite of Spring* and Debussy's *Prélude à l'Après-Midi d'Un Faune*.) A more selfish act it is hard to imagine. It strands the accursed maestro on an island of indecision. To wave or not to wave?

Some choose to wave, not trusting the solo instrument to pick either the right tempo or volume for the passage, and preferring to draw the eyes of the audience to where they rightly belong—on him. There's no denying that this can be an effective *coup de théâtre*, with the audience able to see clearly the relationship between gesture and sound. Besides, with ensemble not a problem, you can make your gestures as fanciful as you like, weaving imaginary spells in the air like a child with a sparkler on bonfire night.

The player, of course, may argue that he is perfectly able to play the passage without your help, from which you must conclude that they

What could be easier? You raise your arm (the right arm only, for the moment. You're not ready to use the left as well. Perhaps you never will be), then lower it. Child's play, no?

No.

For in that simple gesture the pitfalls are many.

Let us play the scene out.

---

are sadly missing the point and unsuitable for further participation in concerts under your direction. The other most commonly used option is to leave the player to their own devices entirely. All that is required is to indicate to him when you feel everyone is ready for the performance to begin. This can take the form of a polite inviting gesture, a raised eyebrow, or, as practised by the great Gnothi Seauton at the beginning of Mahler's Fifth Symphony, a cheeky wink. Taking this act of non-participation to its logical extreme, and, in my opinion, beyond the limits of acceptability, was the conductor, guru and self-confessed charlatan Rothley Cossington. It was his habit, during his mercifully short career, to begin the *Rite of Spring* seated on the floor in the Lotus position. He would hold this pose for up to five minutes, having first ordered the solo bassoonist to wait a preordained time. As the first plaintive note sounded from the by now uncontrollably nervous instrumentalist, he unfolded himself in a convoluted display of terpsichorean self-indulgence, as if enacting one of Twyla Tharp's worst nightmares, rising to his feet in time to 'conduct' the opening bars from the normal position. While this nauseating display may have had the benefit of diverting the audience's attention from the bassoonist, thus marginally relieving the pressure on the poor player, the ultimate effect was to demean and belittle both the music and the player. Given that his conducting was of an equally sordid and sensational nature, it was neither surprising nor displeasing that his career was so short.

You raise your arm. Nothing happens. So far, so good. Nothing is exactly what should be happening at this point.

Your arm reaches the top of its ascent. You decide it might be a good idea to let it fall lest people think you are attempting a one-man Mexican wave. Nothing, that has been happening for a few seconds now, continues to happen. You're still on course.

Your arm begins its descent. This is the crucial phase. You don't want to throw it downwards, otherwise it will reach the bottom before the musicians have had time to react and you run the risk of bashing yourself in a painful area. By the same token, you mustn't hold your arm at the top for too long—the musicians are now in the early stages of being about to think about playing, and the resultant stasis will cause them to hold their breath for an uncomfortably long time. No, merely allow gravity to take its course. Your arm will begin to descend.

You are to imagine a point in the air where you want the sound to come, and aim for that point.

One of two things will happen. In a way that is comparable to the arrival of a baby, the sound will either come earlier than you expected, or later.

It will never come when you expected it. This is a most important basic and immutable law of conducting (and of baby-making, incidentally), and the sooner you accept it, the better.

At this point there are several possibilities:

**1. Your hands reach the point in the air where the sound should come, but it doesn't.**

Option A: Keep your arms still at the bottom and wait for the players to play. This option has a fundamental flaw: it is the players who are waiting for you. There was something so deeply inadequate about your downbeat (and your upbeat, but that's another matter) that they simply didn't think it could have anything to do with the music. It might be best to start again, by which I don't mean the piece, I mean your life.

Option B: Continue to the second beat. This is better than complete stillness, but you run the risk that when you get to the second beat the sound will still not have appeared. Alternatively, it will start at the point in the second beat where it is most off-putting to you. In this case, you will be inhabiting a bizarre parallel universe in which your gestures are totally unrelated to the music in every respect. Don't worry—many people have forged whole careers based on this concept.

Option C: Jiggle your arms about in the hope that someone, somewhere, will interpret it as an invitation to play. This may have some effect, but there are complex mathematical forces at play which will determine whether the music can continue in accordance with your wishes. I don't want to blind you with science, but it might be a good idea to give an outline of these rules below.

There are a number of variables:

$X$ = the number of people in the orchestra.

$Y$ = the number of people who start playing.

$C$ = the 'critical mass' of people playing that must be attained in order for the rest of the orchestra to join in and for the music to continue.

$W$ = woodwind players who play.

$S$ = string players who play.

$B$ = brass players who play.

$P$ = percussionists who play.

Broadly speaking $C$ (the critical mass) can only be attained if the following criteria are met:

$Y > 0.33X$

And any of:

$S > 0.8Y$ or $S + W > 0.7Y$ or $S + W + B > 0.5Y$

There are some absolutes:

$B > W - S$

$B + W > S$

If $Y = P$, then $C$ *is impossible.*

From this we see the following:

For the music to continue, at least a third of the orchestra must play. The makeup of this crucial percentage can vary, but it *must include some string players*.

The more brass or woodwind instruments who play, the fewer people you need to achieve C.

Brass instruments outweigh woodwinds, if no strings play.

Brass instruments plus woodwinds outweigh strings.

Percussion instruments coming in by themselves render the whole exercise meaningless and you must start again.

There are exceptions to the above rules, but by the time you've worked them out you might as well just stop, make an apologetic announcement to the audience, and start again from scratch.

In order to be confident of managing such mishaps, the conductor must commit to memory the above equations. Those interested in studying this subject in greater depth, in which category I include any truly serious conducting student, can find many more rules in the invaluable publication *Mass Hysteria: The Principle of Crowd Dynamics and Suggestibility, its Relevance to Orchestral Practice and its Application in Concert Scenarios* by the acknowledged master of Theoretical Orchestral Psycho-physics Professor Ganz Unmerklich. The conductor must also develop the ability to assess each situation in a speedy and detached manner, and to take the appropriate course of action before further damage is done. Orchestral confusion is like climate change: there is a tipping point, after which anything you do will be disastrous, and your only option is damage limitation.

Of course, given the complexity of the subject, and the controversy surrounding Professor Unmerklich's groundbreaking theories, the conductor's time would be better spent learning how to do it right in the first place.

## 2. The sound arrived much earlier than you thought it would.

In this case, you are actually in serious doo-doo, for the simple reason that the music has started without you.

Imagine you're driving a car. This situation is the equivalent of said car moving off before you've turned the key in the ignition. Your rôle is simply that of a passenger, and the best thing you can do is sit back and look as if you're enjoying the ride, maybe with one hand on the wheel to give the impression to any passing policemen that you're actually in control.

In practical terms, this presents more problems. If you're lucky, you'll be able to catch up with the orchestra and arrange your gestures in line with the music without anyone knowing any better. There is, however, the serious danger, never to be underestimated, of some players actually taking notice of what you're doing and, as it were, 'going rogue' by playing exactly on your beat. If they do this after you've caught up with them, then fine. If before, the only possible result is chaos.

3. The sound arrived at about the right time, but it was atrocious: not together, uncertain, tentative. Certainly not the kind of sound you can take home for Sunday lunch.
That's life in the big city. Count your blessings, live with it, and carry on as normal, hoping that this fragile state of affairs will remain in place for as long as possible.

4. The sound arrived at exactly the right time and was thoroughly acceptable.
This was clearly an accident. Consider retiring while you're still ahead.

H AVING MORE OR LESS successfully started the music, don't for a second believe that your mission has been a success. Professor Ruhiger's reaction to a student who started a piece without life-endangering musical fallout was always the same: 'Unt now you zink you are condectink gut? No! You are condectink rotten, but lucky!'

Besides, now you've started, you have to continue, which brings us neatly to our next section.

# [15]

# *Continuing*

NOW YOU'VE MORE OR LESS started, you have no choice. You must continue.

There are as many ways to continue as there are conductors, but it's generally acknowledged that the process should involve some sort of arm movement.

As always, however, there are exceptions. Before I continue with a technical analysis of the different ways to wave, it would be beneficial to relate the story of one great conductor, his eccentric methodology, and how it nearly contributed to his premature death. It serves as a warning to any young conductor who might be considering refining his gestures that bit too far.

Ignatius 'Gnothi' Seauton was a slim and dapper man, always immaculately turned out, punctual to a fault, and economical in everything he did. Over the course of a fifty-year career as an increasingly popular and in-demand conductor of orchestras just below the top rank, he honed his manual technique to a point where it could best be described as vestigial. Those who knew him as a young man reported that in the early days he was renowned for his wildness on the podium, to the extent that front desk players sometimes feared for their own personal safety. As he grew older, however, he observed that the more he thrashed about the less influence he had on the players. Taking this thought to its logical conclusion, he developed, over several years, a most unusual technique which consisted mostly of doing nothing at all. Without the destabilising influence of erratic gesticulations in their peripheral vision, the players were able to get on with their job. Seauton, meanwhile, kept the carriage on the road, so to speak, with occasional flicks and winks, as well as a rich vocabulary of crowd-pleasing pranks that he would throw in without warning to the orchestra, but at points in the music when he knew they would have no detrimental effect.

As luck had it, I managed to get hold of a returned ticket for what would turn out to be Seauton's final concert, in Athens in 1984. I had heard much about this man who defied all the principles of conventional conducting technique and was keen to observe him for myself in an effort to work out whether he was a genius or a charlatan (the dividing line is often razor-thin). My seat was perfectly positioned for such observations—low down to one side, with a clear view of the great man.

He passed quite close to me on the way to the stage, so I was able to observe at first hand the lengths to which he had gone in his appearance: immaculate patent leather shoes which looked to me like the work of the great Venetian cobbler Gianandrea dello Stronzo; a raw silk Nehru jacket by Armani with matching trousers, the subtle piping no more nor less ostentatious than was necessary; a waft of the unmistakeable scent of *Barfe pour hommes*; and a gently glistening pomade in his distinguished silver hair. As he climbed on to the stage I caught sight not only of crisply ironed cotton double cuffs but solid gold cufflinks.

He hadn't conducted a note, and already I was impressed.

First on the programme was Glinka's *Ruslan and Ludmila Overture*, an orchestral showpiece that, in truth, requires little more from the conductor than the ability to keep up with the orchestra.

To begin the piece, Seauton stood stock still, arms by his sides, chin on chest. Raising his head slowly, but otherwise remaining quite motionless, he held the pose for a few seconds, and then raised his eyebrows twice to indicate the tempo. A shake of the head, and the piece began.

I have never, before nor since, heard an orchestra deliver such whipcrack ensemble and ferocious power at the beginning of this piece. It was as if Seauton, with that single shake of his head, had summoned the forces of Beelzebub and unleashed them in a howling vortex of energy. As the piece blazed its trail Seauton stood calmly in the middle of it, smiling benignly, hands clasped in front of him, like a benevolent wizard monitoring the progress of a spell. A nod, to correct a late oboe entry; a wink, to encourage the horns to a more pungent crescendo. Otherwise he didn't move until the approach of the tempo change near the end of the piece. About ten bars before this critical moment, he slowly and smoothly raised one hand in front of him. Responding instantly to a twitch of the Seauton wrist, the orchestra changed gear as smoothly as a Rolls-Royce Corniche, and the piece roared to a stunning conclusion.

I sat back in my seat, exhausted. The piece had only lasted five minutes, but I felt as if I had been taken on a journey round the world. And all achieved through the most basic concept: an almost total lack of movement. There was no doubt that this was conducting of the highest order.

But if this was conducting, then what had I been doing all these years?

Of the concerto I remember less, possibly because of Post-Traumatic Stress Disorder. The piano soloist, a young Italian who assaulted Tchaikovsky's First Piano Concerto as if it had killed his grandmother, ignored Seauton throughout, a slight that the great Maestro was happy to reciprocate. In doing so, he also obeyed the first rule of accompanying: adopt the opposite demeanour. I barely remember a note of the performance, but have a vivid memory of Seauton's back, turned on the soloist throughout, its every muscle locked in rigid disapproval of the young buck's distressing antics.

Unprofessional? Probably. But needs must when the devil drives a steamroller through your sitting room.

I spent the interval nursing an inferior glass of retsina and contemplating what I had seen. On the one hand, complete mastery; on the other, a distinct lack of professionalism, albeit under the direst provocation. What would the second half bring? My drink may not have been an enticing prospect, but the thought of what Seauton might do with Stravinsky's *Rite of Spring* certainly was.

Everything started conventionally enough. The bassoonist's opening soliloquy rang out loud and clear, apparently unprompted by any movement from Seauton. This was normal enough practice, and of course good psychology. But as the other wind instruments entered and the labyrinthine textures of this elusive music thickened, twining round each other in intricate spirals, he continued to take no part. Not even a flicker crossed his face. Surely it was not possible to play this piece, with its massive orchestra and complex rhythmic structure, without some sort of intervention from the man at the helm? Yet there he stood, unwavering in his refusal to take part. The players seemed perfectly happy with this lack of involvement, and I shouldn't have been surprised after what I had heard in the overture, but this was a completely different proposition. Stravinsky's masterwork contains not only individual parts of great difficulty, but many sudden changes of speed, for which the orchestra relies on strong direction from the front. In addition, the sheer size of the orchestra means that it's almost impossible for all the players to hear each other, necessitating some sort of visual cue. It is a piece in which the conductor can justify his existence (or otherwise). To allow them to negotiate this notorious minefield all on their own was like attempting to cross Niagara Falls on a rickety bicycle without safety net, high wire, or indeed bicycle.

I started to observe Seauton more closely, and thought I detected a pallor in his skin, a lack of focus in his good-natured gaze. Was there something amiss?

As the thought popped into my head, he whipped into action. His head jerked, an elbow pointed, and the orchestra launched itself into the climactic dance of Part One, a gathering whirlwind of orchestral sound which hurls itself forwards and upwards in a relentless surge before throwing itself lemming-like over the edge of the cliff. As the music gathered momentum, Seauton lifted his arms in a smooth gesture, as if picking up the sound and carrying the weight of it in them. The colour had returned to his cheeks and the music had revived with it. He raised his arms gradually higher, finally relinquishing his grip as the music hurtled to its manic conclusion.

Again I was stunned. Against all the odds and with the most unconventional means, Seauton had pulled off the most daring piece of conductorial choreography while at the same time remaining absolutely true to the intentions of the music.

As Part Two began, my anticipation couldn't have been more exquisitely heightened. The opening, with its mysterious chords and sense of quiet foreboding, was beautifully handled by judicious use of the eyebrows and cheek muscles, each change in harmony and texture marked with the utmost control and subtlety. The famous eleven strokes that precede the final Danse Sacrale jolted through his body as if he were being punched in the solar plexus.

And then we were off.

The Danse Sacrale is notoriously complex, cross-rhythms pinging across the orchestra seemingly without pattern, each one dependent on the other. One false step, a momentary hesitation from a single member of the orchestra, and the whole edifice comes tumbling down in ungainly fashion.

The first few bars went well, the irregular rhythms negotiated with surefooted aplomb by the orchestra.

Then, disaster. The timpanist, crucial to the success of the passage, played one note a fraction late. Seauton's head snapped up, and his right arm, hitherto dormant, flailed in the direction of the errant thwacker. But it was too late. His gesture merely served to confuse everyone. The orchestra, unused to such active intervention from their leader, didn't know what to do. Collectively, they hesitated, on the brink of collapse. Somebody would surely come to the rescue? But who?

In that instant I saw in Seauton's face the conductor's mortal enemy: indecision. Fatally, his left arm joined the fray, trying to show a strong beat. The effect was catastrophic—his arms were not in perfect synchronisation, and the orchestra reacted accordingly, each player trying their hardest to play together with something or other, and narrowly failing. The music started to fray at the edges like a teenager's jeans. Seauton, seeking to bring it all together, made the classic rookie's error—he started to make bigger and bigger gestures, punching the air in desperation and flailing in all directions in an effort to bring it all under control. His demeanour began to resemble that of a supply teacher trying to quell a classroom of delinquent fourteen-year-olds. His movements were in direct defiance of anything Stravinsky had written, and completely at odds with what the players were trying to do. The more he thrashed, the less together they played; and the less together they played, the more he tried to put matters right with increasingly frenzied and irrelevant thrashings.

As he fought harder and harder to try to correct the ever-growing pile of rhythmic errors, Seauton began to show signs of physical distress. He had gone pale again, and there was a glassiness in his eyes. The game was up and he knew it. But there was more than that. As the dance lurched its way to a conclusion of sorts, his left hand stopped thrashing and groped for his chest. At the height of the frenzy he sank to his knees, his head hitting the floor at exactly the same moment as the final blow of the piece.

In the shocked aftermath of the performance, nobody in the auditorium moved a muscle. It was as if they had had the air punched out of them.

Then came a tumult of applause and cheering.

The entire auditorium was under the impression that the collapse was part of Seauton's interpretation. Even I, who had been observing him closely, was almost taken in and hesitated to spring up to help only because I feared the great man might jump to his feet to acknowledge the applause as I was about to administer the kiss of life.

Gradually the truth dawned, and there was a flurry of activity as people rushed to help. A doctor was found, and the Maestro was taken to a hospital where a heart attack, 'brought on by sudden and extreme stress', was diagnosed. Although his recovery was swift, he took the decision never to perform again. I am convinced that his retirement was on psychological grounds, not just because of the damage done to his heart. He knew that his own panic had brought on the coronary, and he couldn't risk the chance of it being repeated, with possibly terminal consequences.

Is there a moral to this story? Perhaps.

Gnothi Seauton's expertise was such that he was able to keep his hand on the tiller of virtually any performance without apparent trouble, steering the metaphorical ship through waters deep and shallow with all the calmness of a Zen master on Mogadon. He knew that his finely honed gestures, when he unveiled them, would have even greater effect than if he had been constantly 'beating time', disrupting the course of the craft and giving the passengers an unnecessarily rocky ride. Yet when the boat veered too close to the rocks and crashed into them, he found himself powerless to bring the craft back under control and, like a metaphor stretched beyond its limits, the whole thing floundered in a flurry of flailing and flapping, sinking under the weight of its own alliteration.

Caution: when you conduct, conduct.

HAVING ESTABLISHED THAT beating time is an evil necessity for the vast majority of conductors, I should perhaps give some further information on the corralling of said beating into recognisable patterns.

Most conducting manuals are widthy tomes, replete with diagrams more suited to instructions on how to tie a Windsor knot. I dispense with these diagrams for one simple reason.

I can't draw.

Words are my tools, and for this task I need just four of them: down, up, left, right.

It's very simple:

One is down.

Two is left in four, right in three, and up in two.

Three (in four) is right, but in three, that's wrong. It's up.

Four is up, but in three, two or one, when there is no four (or three or two, respectively), up is three (or two, or one).

Five is two and three or three and two, so it's two lefts and a right or two rights and a left, sandwiched between a down and an up. If you need one more, add a left. Or a right. In a fast 'two and three' five, one (that is the two) is a small down, and two (which is to say the three) is a big up. If it's a 'three and two' five, the one that is the three and the two that is the two are a big down and a small up respectively.

Six is two, except when it's six, when it's five plus one.

But only if you're German.

Seven, eight, nine, ten, eleven and twelve are generally a mixture of twos and threes.

I'm sure you can work them out for yourself.

Avoid anything bigger than twelve. The composer should know better.

If all this is too confusing, here's a simple rule of thumb: after left comes right, except when you're in a five (a three and two five, that is) or more, when right is wrong and further left is right. After that, the only thing left is right, which is right.

And if, even after that concise and lucid explanation, you still find it all a bit much, circles will do fine.

I hope I make myself clear.

# [16]

# *Gestural Vocabulary*

ONCE YOU'VE COMMITTED to memory the simple *aide-mémoire* at the end of the last chapter, the basic mechanical processes of conducting should present you with no problems. These gestures do of course require copious amounts of practice. In order to perfect them, practise in front of a mirror. In order to look like a total git, practise while walking down Lewisham High Street. At all costs, however, avoid practising while standing on a bus. The author accepts no responsibility for any injury caused to innocent passers-by.

The perfection of these gestures in the privacy and silence of your own home is one thing. Application to real life situations is quite another.

The idea may occur to you that to prepare for conducting a real orchestra it would be helpful to practise while listening to a CD.

You should avoid this as assiduously as an antelope avoids a hungry lion.

To understand why, play out the following scene:

Load up one of your favourite tunes—it doesn't matter what it is.

Stand, poised, ready to conduct. When the music starts, (isn't it amazing how it started without you?) wave your arms around in time with it. Notice how good it feels. As the music gets louder and more frenzied, throw yourself around more, to reflect the passion in the music. As it becomes tranquil, stand on tiptoe, a look of bliss on your face, your arms outstretched and barely moving, to reflect the peaceful ecstasy of the passage.

Before the piece finishes, stop your arm-waving and go and masturbate.

You will notice two things:

1. The music miraculously continues without you.

2. The feelings of pleasure brought on by masturbation are similar, if more intense, to the feelings of pleasure brought on by waving your arms around to music that has already been recorded. And, truth be told, you look marginally less ridiculous. So you might as well do that instead and dispense with the arm-waving.

Now that we've got that cleared up, as it were, we can turn our attention to the, ahem, matter in hand. Namely:

## WHAT TO DO WHEN IT GOES WRONG.

Let's not pretend for a second that this isn't going to happen. Most of a conductor's working life is taken up with trying to stop it going wrong and dealing with it when it does, so it's best to get used to the idea and be prepared.

Realistically, when you're beginning to conduct, it's more than likely that your opening gesture will have caused some confusion among the players. The confusion may even have set in some time before that, as you entered the room or ascended the podium. In extreme situations, even the sight of your name on the roster will have engendered a reaction of 'What the...?'

Don't worry—this is perfectly normal.

What you need now is some sort of corrective measure.

Here are some of the more common ways of dealing with the fallout generated by a faulty opening gesture, and some of the inherent problems contained therein.

The 'Bugger It's Too Fast' Over-compensation
(BITFOC)

Very common, this one. In your understandable nerv-
ousness, you have ignored the first rule of starting a
piece: 'Try to remember what speed the music goes
before you begin.' As a result, the opening sounds rather hurried. Your thought processes might go something like this:

Thought 1: 'Hold on, I recognise that.'

Thought 2: 'Woah Nelly, now I know what it is!'

Thought 3: 'Crikey, why are they playing it so
fast?'

Thought 4: 'Oh. I see.'

Thought 5: 'Better do something about it then, I
suppose.'

The problem with the resulting gesture, which resembles nothing more than a flightless bird trying to
defy gravity and evolution simultaneously, is that it
simply gets in the way. The damage is done. The orchestra have already gone off at the speed you gave
them with your first gesture. Too late now, mate. If
you wave your arms slower, half of them will go with
you, and the other half will stay the same speed. The
music will die, and it will be your fault.

Music-murderer. Blood on your hands. Shame on
you.

## The 'Aargh! Half Speed! No!' Utter Panic Flap (AHSNUPF)

You have tried to make your opening gesture encompass all the music, as you've been taught. Overdoing it slightly, you give a gesture that makes you look as if you're carrying a large round table downstairs. The resultant sound is reminiscent of the soundtrack to the film *Inception*.

Desperate to correct the situation, you engage the AHSNUPF. It makes you look as if you've dropped the table on your toe and are now trying to catch a very large frog.

## The 'A Bit Fast?' Accelerating Beat (ABFAB)

You've started too fast. Giddy with the excitement of it all, you decide to go even faster. This is marginally better than the BITFOC, with one major drawback. The players can't play the notes. Oh well. Tough. You're having fun listening to them try.

## The 'Getting-It-All-Going-Again' Thrash (GIAGAT)

There are some pieces that just can't seem to get moving. You thought you gave a good upbeat, but the orchestra don't appear to have read the memo. Wary of lapsing too soon into the AHSNUPF (see above), you bide your time and try to ease the tempo forwards until it resembles something the audience might recognise. This delicate operation is hindered by the fact that the players, having lost faith in your competence the moment you raised your arms (or even earlier), are now ignoring you with all the doggedness of a traffic warden ignoring the protests of someone who has 'only stopped there for a couple of minutes, honest.'

Desperate to grab their attention, you make faster and larger gestures, in the hope that they will be clearer.

Wrong.

It just looks as if you are drowning.

Which, in a sense, you are.

## The 'Ok You Know Best' Accompanying Gesture (OYKBAG)

In all of the above situations, you're clearly trying to do what is best for the music, and there's no shame in that. But if life teaches us anything, it's that sometimes pragmatism is the best policy.

It's time to deploy the OYKBAG.

Bowing to the inevitable, you allow the orchestra to do what it does naturally—play together. Listen carefully and try to make your gesture look as if it's related to the tempo of the music—this is not as easy as it looks.

164

To be brutally frank, the sooner you can rid your-self of encumbrances like the BITFOC, AHSNUPF, ABFAB and GIAGAT, and submit to successful deployment of the OYKBAG, the better. The last thing the musicians want is to be distracted by a demented traffic cop making signals that blatantly contradict the character, tempo and style of the music.

Remember, a good conductor should be like a good football referee: do the job well and nobody will even know you're there.

AFTER A BIT EVERYTHING settles down, and the musicians remember that the conductor is like the national speed limit: everyone ignores it, but it's comforting to know it's there. They can now get on with the business of driving safely (listening to each other and playing together) while occasionally slowing down to sixty-eight mph (watching the conductor) when they see a police car (when they think he's looking).

This process will no doubt engender in you a feeling of satisfaction, possibly even euphoria. You're conducting! You're really conducting!!

Or at least you think you are, which amounts to very much the same thing.

At this point you might feel the need to make your presence felt with some added gestures. You don't want, after all, to be one of those conductors who is known as simply an 'efficient time-beater'. You want to imbue the music with meaning.

Here are some tried and tested favourites:

### The Broad Horizontal Sweep
### (known in the U.K. as the 'four runs')

Used when the music is lyrical and expansive, this is the universal symbol for 'Make more sound'. Usually accompanied by a slight forward and leftward lean, it more often than not has the unintended and detrimental effect of making the music go slightly faster.

### The 'A.O.K. Staccato Jab'

The thumb and first finger of the left hand form a circle; the other fingers point upwards, slightly splayed. A sharp jab is executed as rhythmically as the conductor can manage while maintaining a steady beat with the right hand (which, let's face it, is not very). It is intended to denote that individual notes should be played short. It looks more like someone playing darts. Taken in isolation, this hand shape can be misinterpreted as meaning 'Everything's ok!', except in Brazil, where it can be misinterpreted as meaning 'Go fuck yourself!'

## The 'More Expression' Left Hand Flemble

A cross between a flap and a tremble, this gesture is designed to encourage a more expressive style of playing. Unfortunately, as the co-ordination required to execute the gesture takes up all of the conductor's available memory, it usually results in stasis of the right hand, and mild collapse of the music.

It also, like so many of the gestures listed here, doesn't really mean or achieve anything.

## Playing An Imaginary Violin

When the Flemble fails to produce the desired intensity, the conductor dispenses with actual conducting and instead stands hunched over an imaginary violin, possibly with fists clenched. Those playing actual violins look on with bemusement.

## The Mexican Wave

Down. Up. Wahay!

Great for the end of Stravinsky's *Firebird*.

## 'I Give You My Bleeding Heart On A Platter'

Only suitable if you are established as a conductor of the extremely emotional kind, such as the 'Wild Man of Borneo' or 'The Brooder', this gesture can take many forms. All of them are characterised by a rictus-like facial expression and staring eyes. Juddering outstretched arms add to the impression of openness and vulnerability.

### 'Quieter Quieter No Even Quieter Still Quieter' Jazz Hands Down Low

To be accompanied by the kind of expression you get when you suck on a lemon while someone takes out your toenails, this gesture also resembles the furtive shushing you give someone who is about to really put their foot in it in a social situation.

### The 'You Shouldn't Have Played There' Shimmy

This is usually directed at a player who has been sitting around doing nothing for a while and has lost his place. This is emphatically the composer's fault for not giving him enough to do, and has nothing to do with him playing 'Angry Birds'. Definitely not.

Thinking he recognises a cue from the second clarinet, he hastily picks up his instrument and starts playing.

Loudly. In a quiet bit.

The conductor, sensing something is wrong, but not sure exactly what, looks up, sees guilty trombonist (let's say—it's just a hypothetical example, for pity's sake) and gives 'em the shimmy.

The shimmy requires co-ordination: the left hand must clearly send the message to the errant player

'You've come in two bars early, but it's ok, we all make mistakes, now just keep calm and start the next bit, you know, the one starting with the rising diminished fifth...HERE!'; the right hand must continue conveying flowing rhythm and expression to the rest of the orchestra as if nothing untoward was going on. The effect should resemble an expert *maître d'* removing a fly from a customer's wine glass while diverting his attention with a well directed compliment about his tie.

It usually looks more like a startled man hiding a pornographic magazine from his wife.

'I've Got Your Balls In My Left Hand And I'm Gonna Squeeeeeze'
A good stand-by for when the music gets really grindy.

The 'Hunka-Chunka'
Patented by the great Leonard Bernstein, this is a relaxed and repeated shrugging of the shoulders that resembles a slow-motion version of Mike Yarwood's impersonation of Edward Heath, circa 1975. Accompanied by a 'groovy' face, this is only suitable for advanced Leonard Bernsteins. Everyone else who tries to do it looks atrocious.

Spearing the Cherry Tomato
Self-explanatory, I hope.

# [17]

# *Stopping*

IF YOU HAVE DILIGENTLY READ and absorbed the previous chapters, you will by now be reasonably well equipped (in the most basic way imaginable—let's not get ahead of ourselves) to start and continue a piece of music.

There is, of course, only one thing left.

Stopping.

*DISCLAIMER: stopping the music is a high-risk activity. The author accepts no responsibility for personal injury induced by incorrect execution of the following gestures. If in doubt, consult a physician.*

There are several basic kinds of stop.

### The Pause
Pauses present many problems for the novice. You have to stop the music. That in itself is hard enough. But then you have to start it again. It's like a pit stop

in a Grand Prix. Get it wrong and you'll have some-one's leg off.

Let's analyse a common problem, and the chaos that can ensue if correct precautions aren't taken.

Problem: you're unsure whether to slow down into the pause. The players, watching like hawks that have been to Specsavers, reach their own conclusions: half slow down, half don't.

Result: the aural equivalent of a long jumper stuttering at the end of his run-up as he tries to avoid overstepping, followed by the inevitable anguished flurry of metaphorical arms, legs and sand as he ploughs into the metaphorical pit.

The uncertainty continues when you try to escape the pause. Your 'Sustain This Chord' gesture doesn't help—half the orchestra think it's a cut-off. Nor does your hysterical 'Ok Then, Let's Cut Off The Chord' gesture—the rest of them think it's an upbeat. You resort to a series of jerky movements, each one more ambiguous than the last—they merely deepen the befuddlement that now cloaks the orchestra like a blanket of smog. Your misery is compounded by the oboist, the only person who should be playing on your upbeat, coming in half a bar after everyone else.

Solution: produce, at the first rehearsal, 'authentic' evidence that the autograph contains no pause at this point. Even if this means forging a facsimile page of the score, it's easier than conducting what the composer wrote.

### The Actual Pause That You Can't Get Out Of By Producing Faked Evidence
Oh all right then.

Sometimes you have to bow to the inevitable and actually conduct the pause as written. This presents difficulties.

Stopping shouldn't be too hard. You just stop moving at the allotted time. Let's say it's on the fourth beat. You beat one-two-three-ffffffffff, stopping at the bottom of the beat.

Starting again is the problem. If you're not careful, your desire for clarity will involve giving three extra (and entirely unnecessary) gestures plus a twitchy flurry to indicate that those who haven't come in should have come in, and those who have, shouldn't have.

So to avoid this, don't stop in the first place. Rather, keep moving through the fourth beat, but at such a retarded rate that it will at first seem as if you are reenacting one of the key scenes from *The Matrix*. When you feel the pause has gone on long enough, and pausing only to pluck a speeding bullet from the air in front of you, give a little flick and continue to the first beat as normal.

The only danger with this manoeuvre is that if the pause is too long and your rate of movement too fast, your hands may escape the orbit of your body, with embarrassing and possibly harmful consequences.

Keep the pause short, and all you have to do is twitch just as it reaches breaking point, and the music can continue.

Another handy technique is to delegate responsibility of the breaking of the pause to the leader of the orchestra.

### The Timed Pause

Sometimes a modern composer will request that a pause last a certain length of time. You know the ones. A pause of ten or fifteen seconds, during which individual instruments enter in turn as directed by the conductor while the cellos play an improvised repeating phrase based on the shape of a squiggly line. These are best negotiated by resorting to the traffic cop approach ('Play when I point at you') with the left hand while keeping the right hand entirely still.

They are also best negotiated by making them, at most, half the length of what is designated. Otherwise the music, already unutterably tiresome, becomes actively harmful to presumably innocent bystanders.

## The End

All good things must end. Even Mahler (eventually).

Picture the scene. The performance has gone swimmingly and you're approaching the climax, surfing waves of euphoria that will transport audience and orchestra alike to new levels of exhilaration, their lives transformed by the insights your conducting brings to the music.

There's only one problem.

You don't know how to stop.

Regardless of the practicalities of negotiating the final bars, you have two options when it comes to your final position:

1. If the music finishes loudly: stiff, outstretched arms; eyes closed in exultation; mouth open; decisive forehand to finish (topspin or slice optional), triumphant/shattered smile/glazed expression (delete as appropriate, according to mood of ending).

2. If the music finishes quietly: exaggeratedly long silence after the final chord, eyes closed as mark of deep emotion, lips slightly parted; eventual tired but reverential lowering of arms.

N.B. These are not optional.

As the applause begins, a relieved smile and nodding head are usual. These purport to mean 'Well done everyone, you were great', but actually mean 'Well done me. I'm great, aren't I?'

# [18]

# *Cueing*

A s you progress on your conductorly way, there will be times when players ask questions.

Don't panic.

It's usually not the answer that's important, but the firmness with which it's delivered. All that's required is a brief perusal of the relevant spot in the score, then a businesslike 'Piano', 'Staccato' or 'G#', as if you have given the matter lengthy thought, but have more important things to worry about.

Sidebar 1: if a player asks about dynamics, the answer is always 'Piano'.

Sometimes, though, the question is terrifyingly specific.

'Er, sorry, Maestro, but could you possibly cue us at figure 28?'

Sidebar 2: beware the musician who calls you 'Maestro', especially with an audible capital 'M'. They rarely mean it as a compliment. Remember that the Maestro was a cheap and nasty car that was especially prone to rust and unpleasant emissions.

There may be excellent reasons for the request, but be careful. Firstly, it's possible that the player in question isn't even playing at figure 28 and is just toying with you. Secondly, in trying to fulfil the request, you risk neglecting all other aspects of the music from figure 25 onwards and conducting like an automaton.

In extreme cases, the musicians may even notice.

The cue should be a reminder to the player, an acknowledgement, an unspoken manifestation of the telepathy that unifies instrumentalist and conductor in their unremitting quest for musical perfection. This ideal is undermined when the conductor delivers the cue with an autocratic flap, like a peer of the realm directing a plumber to the tradesmen's entrance. The conductor should, *au contraire*, execute the cue lovingly, with an elegant unfurling of the left hand, as if inviting a beautiful lady to the dance floor. More often they propel it at the benighted player like Dutch arrows master Raymond van Barneveld throwing the last leg of a nine-dart finish.

There are four basic cues:

# Cueing

### The Unwitting Early Cue

There will be occasions when a player has an important entry after a long rest. The thoughtful conductor should give him a glance, a few bars ahead, to check that he is (a) upright, (b) awake, (c) alive.

If a-c above apply, he may see you looking at them and, ignoring every musical instinct, start playing.

Two bars early.

Standard procedure is for the conductor to try to correct this, causing the player to start the entry again.

Two bars late.

If a-c do not apply, there is nothing you can do.

In fact, 'There is nothing you can do' serves as a useful motto for life in general, and should be engraved on conductor's stands everywhere.

### The On-Time Cue

They were going to play anyway, but the conductor feels better for having noticed.

### The Late, or 'Reactive' Cue

The conductor has his head in the score. The instrument plays. The conductor hears it, looks up, and gives the player a little flap. At best this is taken to mean 'Ah, there you are. Jolly good. Carry on.' At worst he will stop playing.

## The Misdirected Cue

The conductor, remembering that there is a massive and dramatic timpani cue coming up, conducts in an understated manner for the ten bars before it. Then, with a theatrical flourish, he whips round and directs his finest and most triumphant gesture towards the timpani.

Unfortunately he has forgotten that, because of an unusually cramped stage, the timpanist is sitting on the other side of the orchestra, so the recipient of his grand gesture is a befuddled harpist who is not playing in this movement.

IN SUMMARY, CUES ARE more trouble than they're worth. A good tactic is to eschew them altogether. Alternatively, you can cue continuously in a general kind of way by swivelling your torso in the vague direction of a group of players, but (and this is the important part) only when they aren't playing. This, however, is an advanced technique best left to seasoned professionals. Don't worry if you can't master it. The music will carry on quite nicely without you.

# [19]

# *The Stick*

A CONDUCTOR'S CHOICE of baton (or 'stick' in the vernacular) can be the source of much hand-wringing and indecision as the inexperienced conductor agonises over what might seem to the outsider quite a trivial matter.

But the choice of stick is so crucially and inextricably linked to the general subject of the conductor's image that this dilemma is quite understandable. The variety of options is bewildering. Batons are made to many different specifications: length, weight and balance are key properties whose variability can affect a conductor's feel for the music either to its advantage or its detriment. The material of both shaft and handle, and their shape and feel in the hand, can be crucial factors in the conductor's grasp of the sound—somewhat akin to the violinist's bow, the snooker player's cue, or the commercial pleasure worker's cat o' nine tails.

Do you, for example, opt for the 'Henry Wood' style? The great man used a two-foot stick of the kind you might use to roast a suckling pig, and of course backed up his choice with an equally impressive (and daily sharpened) beard. This stick, woefully out of fashion nowadays, may denote a conductor of the 'old school', so you should think carefully about your clothes, making sure they precisely match your choice of stick. A tweed three-piece suit would not be inappropriate, and you may even consider using a shooting stick in place of a stool in rehearsal.

Going to the opposite extreme, you may wish to eschew the baton altogether, in the style of many great and sensitive conductors. Indeed, it is that sensitivity that is often associated with 'stickless' wagglers, the impression they give being of one able to hold the music close to them and mould it to their will. The 'sticky' conductor may be a wizard, standing slightly aloof from the music and musicians and directing them with their wand; the 'stickless' is more akin to a chef, not afraid to reach into the stinking bowels of the music and haul out a handful of offal.

There was no greater exponent of the stickless style than the incomparable Lebanese conductor, Bashir 'Baba' Ganoush. Ganoush was sadly cut off at the des-

perately young age of thirty-five by the brutal and in-
felicitous combination of a vigorous daily exercise routine and a weak hotel balcony. But in the ten years of
his sparkling ascendancy, he set new standards for ba-
ton-free conducting. The image I hold in my head is of
Ganoush standing with his hands cupped, head leaning
forward and slightly to the right, as if cradling a chick
and straining to hear what it had to say. From this
would grow a variety of fascinating and expressive gestures as he kneaded, squeezed, sprinkled, flicked and
caressed the last drops of music out of the orchestra. In
lyrical passages his hands swooped through the air like
a flock of starlings. But he was not afraid to exhibit
more masculine qualities when necessary, his slim
frame somehow growing and his fists balled pugna-
ciously to match the size of the music. In Prokofiev's
'The Death of Tybalt' from *Romeo and Juliet*, for example, it was almost as if he was enacting the fight
himself, each parry and thrust perfectly matched to the
nuance of the music. And in more delicate passages it
sometimes seemed as if the music actually took flight
under his fluttering fingers.

Like anyone, of course, Ganoush had his detractors.
Accused of lacking rhythm by a bold percussionist one
night in the bar after a mesmerising, if precarious,
performance of Bartók's *Concerto for Orchestra*, Ganoush simply replied 'You must pay more attention to

the little finger of my left hand.' And when asked by a presumptuous horn player if he could furnish them with a clear downbeat for a particularly tricky chord in Sibelius's Fifth Symphony, Ganoush retorted irritably 'Downbeats are for robots. Watch closely and the meaning of the music will become clear.'

Such flexibility of expression is by no means solely the preserve of conductors who eschew the baton, as anyone who witnessed the work of the incomparable Italian conductor Stinco di Maiale can testify. Di Maiale (or 'Stinky' as he was inevitably and fondly known in this country) was the epitome of latinate suaveness and charm, and to see him in full flow with his 60-centimetre stick was an unforgettable experience. In his hands the stick shimmered and shone, its tip delineating expressive lines of, simultaneously, the utmost complexity and simplicity. It was as if angels were performing trapeze acts from it. The music spoke through his stick. Many was the performance in which we would sit mesmerised by the sheer beauty of the man and his miraculous shaft. Sometimes it wasn't even necessary to listen to the music—he was a one-man podium ballet.

When asked how he achieved his magic, he would lean in to the questioner, give a sly wink and confide 'When I conduct, I draw beautiful woman in air.'

*The Stick*

Di Maiale's demise was part tragedy, part comedy. During a performance of Ravel's *Daphnis et Chloé*, his aerial acrobatics became particularly florid and ornate, leading to an unfortunate spearing of his left hand. He continued as if nothing had happened, his gestures becoming, if anything, more extravagant, and spraying blood over orchestra and audience alike. His casual attitude to the wound persisted after the concert. He waved away suggestions that he should seek medical attention, preferring to show it off to all and sundry at the after-concert party and regarding it as an honestly gained war wound.

He contracted septicæmia and died six days later.

## Stick Technique

THE TERM 'STICK TECHNIQUE' may usually be taken to refer to the manual method of using a baton, its honing and perfection until the conductor is able to express what he wants, when he wants.

I use it here in its alternative meaning: namely, how to use the subject of batons to undermine, or 'stick it to', your rivals.

On the thankfully rare occasions when you rub shoulders with other conductors, it's crucial that you

185

establish the upper hand early on. One example of an 'in the field' encounter will suffice to demonstrate the importance of this principle.

Two conductors meet, and are talking shop. The conversation, having naturally touched on all manner of subjects (but mostly the relative successes of the two conductors, each trying to outdo the other with tales of their achievements and the nonchalance with which they are told) turns to batons.

Conductor A: You still using the old faithful?

Conductor B: Never felt any need to change. My hand's got used to it. Got myself a decent supply when I was in Hong Kong the other month with the ballet.

Conductor A: Try one of these. Got it made by this fantastic chap in Great Yarmouth. Zebrawood handle, Estonian birch for the shaft.

Conductor B (weighing it in his hand): Nice heft. What length?

Conductor A: Fourteen and three-eighths. The extra eighth just gives you that little bit more...you know...whip. It's got a lovely pianissimo, but plenty of oomph for the big passages. Lovely Beethoven stick.

Conductor B (trying a few moves, dubiously): I don't know...seems...

Conductor A: What?

Conductor B: Well...obviously it's very personal...but...don't you have trouble really extracting a proper legato? It's just a bit...wooden.

Conductor A (defensive): Really? Hadn't noticed.

Conductor B: Well, of course, if you're happy with it...

Conductor A (now doubtful): Well I wouldn't say happy...it's still early days.

Conductor B: I mean, without a really good stick you're never going to get a proper legato...I mean really smooth.

Notice how Conductor B has established his superiority in a very subtle way, implying that not only the stick is wooden (of course it is) but that by association its owner is too.

This approach can be adapted to almost any situation. You may, for example, choose to adopt a devil-may-care attitude, countering your companion's (other conductors are never friends) obsession with stick weight and flex with a display of withering scorn for those who obsess about such details.

Conductor A: So what stick are you using these days?

Conductor B: You know what? All this stick business...it just gets in the way. Sometimes you just have to roll up your sleeves and get your hands dirty. None of this pussyfooting around. Just...(makes expressive gesture with hands, as if kneading bread)...you know?

Conductor A: Well...I...

Conductor B: I want to feel the sound. I want to caress it, mould it, nurture it. Hot damn, man, I want to shag it. And you don't get to do that by holding a lifeless bit of wood in your hand, I can tell you.

Conductor A: (taken aback) Er...really...? You mean you're not using...?

Conductor B: (with a wink) That's right. I'm 'unprotected' these days. Might not be as safe, but sure as hell is more fun.

Rule of thumb: put the other person on the wrong foot early and then push gently.

# PSYCHOLOGICAL ASPECTS

# [20]

# *Players*

ORCHESTRAL MUSICIANS ARE COMPLICATED. Not as complicated as you, obviously. It takes a special breed to become a conductor.

But the handling of them does, nonetheless, require some forethought, especially in these days of 'player power'. Gone is the era when you could just stand there and shout at them. Players nowadays demand, and deserve, a little more respect. They are, after all, the ones making the sound. And with that comes power.

Never forget: without the musicians, you're just an idiot waving your arms around.

I've tried to avoid an abundance of statistics in this book, but here's one that might be of use. In a survey conducted by the Institute of Higher Orchestral Studies in the small town of Zart Hervortretend in Bavaria, it was proven that 98.37% of the time, orchestras do not need conductors in order to perform their duties successfully.

98.37% of the time.

So in a Mahler symphony of, say, ninety minutes, you'll be doing approximately eighty-eight seconds of effective work.

A sobering thought.

They also concluded (although this is more subjective) that an orchestra in full flow will actually improve with the removal of the conductor.

I will never forget the perfect demonstration of this principle in practice. Meerven Westelbeer was a Flemish conductor who carved a niche for himself for a while in the 1970s. His relationship with a certain English orchestra was fuelled by a healthy and mutually malevolent disrespect, and perpetuated only because of the gripping electricity between them that led to many memorable performances. It resembled in this regard a marriage based on conflict, with the inevitable passions that this can engender.

There came a time, however, when the relationship was stretched to the limit, and the collaboration had to end.

The catalyst for this fatal rupture was a performance of Beethoven's *Eroica Symphony*, of which Westelbeer was a renowned interpreter.

He walked to the podium to warm applause. The audience settled down, ready for the performance. Westelbeer, as was his habit, shot his cuffs and brought his arms slowly up to the 'ready' position, a ritual which became more and more prolonged as his career went on, and one which was designed to heighten the audience's anticipation of the forthcoming special event.

When he was no more than one quarter of the way through this ritual, the concertmaster lifted his violin, and led the orchestra in the two E♭ chords that open the piece.

Westelbeer was completely outmanœuvred. In his shock and confusion, he had little option. To stop the piece and insist on starting again would have left him looking petty and ill-tempered. To smile benignly and allow the musicians to carry on would have been the canny thing to do, but it was altogether understandable that he failed, in the circumstances, to think of it. In the event he was all but forced to join in, and this he did, half-heartedly waving for a while, and then trying to give the impression that he was in charge.

But it was too late. The fiction had been exposed like a losing number on a scratchcard, and his gestures, unlike Jeffrey Archer, lacked conviction. Strangely, however, the performance continued with irresistible power, the players committing themselves to the music like never before, and leaving Westelbeer floundering in their wake.

At the end of an exhilarating first movement, Westelbeer looked warily round, as if expecting the players to start without him again. But they knew better—they sat, waiting for him to start the second movement, everything seemingly as normal. Westelbeer went through his routine again, preparing the atmosphere for the solemnity of the Marche Funèbre.

It was his unfortunate practice to start this movement, and others like it, with his eyes closed, the idea being that by doing this he would somehow channel the extreme depth and spirituality of the piece more effectively.

Gravely, he gave the upbeat; a mere twitch.

Silence.

Unperturbed, he tried again; this time, more of a jiggle.

Silence.

Trying to disguise the fact that all was not going to plan, he gave a more vigorous and unequivocal gesture, as if trying to jolt the second violins into action.

Still silence.

Westelbeer had no option. He opened his eyes and looked around him.

Every last player in the orchestra sat, ready to play, but, in obvious deference to the Maestro's example, with their eyes firmly closed.

The rest of the performance followed a predictable pattern. Westelbeer, for the most part, looked on as helplessly as an incompetent referee trying to take charge of a football match played by rebellious multi-millionaires. At one point it seemed as if he was really conducting, but belief deserted him and the slump of his shoulders at the end told its own story, even to the least sensitive of audients.

The performance, for the record, was one of the most successful I have heard.

HOW THEN CAN THE ASPIRING CONDUCTOR avoid such disasters?

Quite simply: understand your position in the complex food chain that is an orchestra. There are some conductors who plopped out of the jelly mould of creation with an authoritative demeanour. They lead naturally, command respect without effort, and enjoy the loyal subservience of understanding and grateful players.

If you're one of those, congratulations. You will do well.

But you're not. Admit it now and your life will be much easier.

The equation is simple: the control exerted by a conductor over a group of players is inversely proportional to the effort he puts into exerting said control.

Learn to live with this stark fact and you stand a chance of survival. A slim one, admittedly, but even that's better than nothing.

# [21]

# *Soloists*

MUCH AS YOU MIGHT HATE the idea, it's occasionally necessary to share the limelight. Audiences
and orchestras cannot subsist on an unvaried diet of
orchestral music alone; they need some leavening.

Enter the soloist.[1]

From the austerity of Vivaldi's *Four Seasons* to the
more muscular charms of a Rachmaninov piano con-

---

[1] There are of course concertos featuring two or more soloists, some
of which have entered the regular repertoire. Consider, however,
eschewing the obvious Mozart, Beethoven and Brahms offerings in
favour of more outré combinations. The appeal of Desto Besser's
*Dithyramb XIX* for piccolo, contrabassoon, Jews' harp and orchestra
may not be immediately apparent, but you'd be surprised at the
number of players of those instruments willing to attend such a performance, and at the distance they're prepared to travel to indulge in
such dubious pleasures.

certo, the presence of a soloist adds interest, value and quite often a sparkly dress to any concert programme.

From the conductor's point of view, a concerto is a mixed blessing. As well as the yielding of the stage to a competing entity, there are technical issues to consider. We have all attended performances that have been at least partially spoiled by a conductor's inability to keep up with a soloist, never pausing to entertain the possibility that it might be the other way round, and that the benighted conductor is merely attempting to restrain a runaway stallion with a loop of dental floss.

So the conductor in a concerto is like the referee in an omelette-throwing contest: under-appreciated, in the line of fire and more than likely to end up with egg on his face.

How is it possible, then, to emerge from the ordeal unscathed, and appearing to present your interpretative partner in the best possible light, while at the same time subtly conveying to those able to see that this one's a bit of a loose cannon?

The first thing to deal with is Concerto Stagecraft.

In this department it's a good idea to tailor your style to that of the soloist. If they're of the extrovert type, swooping and swaying this way and that in a blatant attempt to cover up the fact that they can't play the notes, make a point of staying stock still throughout the performance and muting your gestures to the point that you resemble Fritz Reiner on Mogadon.

'All very well, this showmanship,' your disapproving back will say to the audience, 'but isn't it rather distracting? A bit of inner calm never hurt anybody.'

If, by contrast, the soloist displays an aloof quality of chilly austerity, your aim should be to imply that their restrained attitude is somewhat lacking in simple human warmth. A cheerfully extrovert approach to the accompaniment will suffice, rather than an all-out razzamatazz attack; just enough to convey to the orchestra at least an implication of 'Come on chaps, we've got a bit of a frosty one here—let's ginger it up a touch!' Playing to the audience would be *de trop*, although if the slow movement is of openly sentimental quality, the classic 'head thrown to one side, rapt attention etched into face' pose, just to show how in tune you are with the soloist, is permissible.

When it comes to the execution of the piece itself, a sliding scale comes into play. Luckily there are some works that are very straightforward, requiring little more exertion and stress for the conductor and soloist than would be expended making a Parmesan soufflé, and yielding similar results: technically much easier than they sound, but endlessly impressive to people who know no better.

But then there are pieces that demand all the acrobatics and nerve of a high wire act. The solo part abounds with complexities which are more than matched in the orchestra, and this brings an inevitable danger to both ensemble and balance.

When faced with such a piece, you have two options:

1. Fake your own death.

2. Knuckle down, learn the bloody thing and do the best job you can.

Yielding to the inevitable with a sigh, you will find that passages of apparent complexity are little more than an uneven battle between soloist and orchestra, the former's acrobatics accompanied by the occasional interjection from the latter, like a grumpy uncle watching a child do somersaults and saying 'Not bad, but now do another one' with a surly and grudging nod. As a result, exchanges between soloist and orchestra can sound something like this:

Soloist: tum-tiddle-iddle-skiddle-diddly-twiddly-jiggety-tum-tiddly-squee-tiddly-squaw-tiddly-tiddly-tiddly-squeeeeee.

Orchestra: Bimp. Bomp.

Soloist: rummmmmmm-tiddle-tiddle-tiddle-tiddle (warming to the task) taggedy-taggedy-taggedy-taggedy-riddle-iddle-iddle-iddle-iddle-iddle-iddle-iddle-iddle-iddle-eeeeeeeeeeee.

Orchestra: Bomp. Bimp.

And so on.

For the conductor such exchanges present little problem as long as the bomps and bimps come after a conveniently telegraphed squee or tiddle-om.

The trouble begins when you have to place a bomp (or a bimp, or even a ta-dee) in the context of a continual onslaught of tiddles (or taggedys). This necessitates very careful timing of the upbeat so that the ta-daa (or similar) comes exactly on time and doesn't stagger in, embarrassed and dishevelled, just behind the soloist, in the manner of a student arriving late for a lecture because he's overslept and is still putting his clothes on while entering the lecture theatre.

Older readers will understand when I compare the sense of peril engendered by such manœuvres to sprinting at full speed down Piccadilly and jumping onto a moving No. 9 bus. In these impoverished days of universal Health and Safety, however, I fear the analogy will be lost on those under the age of thirty-five.

Luckily, though, the general course of a concerto consists of the soloist indulging in showoffery of a more or less masturbatory nature, to a backdrop of choom-choom-choom-choom-choom-chugga-dum accompaniment. Occasionally an oboe or some such faux-melodic instrument will pipe up with an answering phrase, only to be put firmly (and quite rightly) in its place by the true centre of attention. The audience, after all, has come to hear the one in the sparkly dress (or affectedly casual raw silk smoking jacket, depending on gender), and they don't want hoi polloi muscling in on the act.

The true nightmare scenario for the conductor is the 'interpretative' soloist. For such players the written text of the piece is not enough, and they feel they have to imbue the music with extra meaning. This usually takes the form of wild lurches in tempo between one bar (or sometimes note) and the next. These variations will invariably differ in concert from what was rehearsed in the afternoon, and result in a pervasive feeling of seasickness in all those present.

I'm being mischievous, of course. Truth to tell, it's the conductor's responsibility to accompany the soloist on every inch of the journey, so blame for these mishaps falls squarely on his slender shoulders.

The music nearly grinds to a halt or falls apart?

Conductor's fault.

Orchestra fails to come in after the blindingly fast scale at the end of a Beethoven piano concerto cadenza?

Conductor's fault.

Soloist completely cacks up the filigree passagework in the last movement?

Conductor's fault.

Take these examples and use them as a stick with which to beat yourself. You are not worthy. You, after all, are merely wiggling vaguely in time with the music. It's the soloist who has to play all the notes. The least you can do is give him the time to play the blasted things.

Inevitably, and much more so than in a performance of a purely orchestral work, the concerto finishes with congratulatory smiles all round, no matter what atrocities have been perpetrated on the music. Flowers are presented, cheeks kissed, and you accompany your colleague off the stage.

Give them a hug. They deserve it.

# [22]

# *Choirs*

Avoid.

# [23]

# *Opera*

THE OPERA CONDUCTOR is a special breed. He must be able to cope with adversity, unwanted surprises, and singers.

The three often go hand in hand.

As if the glorious unpredictability of a hundred obsessive-compulsives wasn't enough, add to the orchestra a group of egomaniacal narcissists and a director whose artistic temperament is at least a match for yours, and you have a recipe for disaster.

It's not so much that things can go wrong in opera, more that they will. It's a statistical certainty. There are just too many factors thrown into the cauldron.

Take, as a perfectly random example, Act Two of Puccini's *La Bohème*.

This, for those who are not familiar with the opera, is a scene set on the bustling streets around the Café

Momus in turn-of-the-century Paris. It involves, according to the score, 'a vast, motley crowd'.

Four words designed to strike cold fear into the heart of a conductor.

When God wants to vex us, She doesn't send hurricanes, tsunamis or locustial plagues—She merely asks us to conduct a crowd scene in an opera.

There's nothing wrong with a crowd *per se*. Crowds are as capable of making beautiful music as individuals are. But in a bustling scene such as the one set in Café Momus, where the thronging streets of Paris must be brought to thrilling life for the benefit of an expectant audience, then the problems begin.

To convey this swarming bustle it stands to reason that the crowd must mill. While milling, they have to sing.

Together.

You can't mill and sing together simultaneously. It's like being Piers Morgan and being likeable—they're mutually exclusive.

It's one thing being in a crowd and singing if you're standing facing the conductor—quite another when you're trying to walk round a crowded stage avoiding grubby street urchins whose remit is to dash around trying to break your neck. And when a single missed entry, even by a split second, will send the whole edifice tumbling down to the floor, never to be reconstructed, the results can only be imagined. Or, if you've ever attended a less-than-perfect production of *La Bohème*, experienced.

In the midst of all the hustle and bustle, of course, a coherent scene must be played out. There is the burgeoning love of the (SPOILER ALERT) ill-fated couple Rodolfo and Mimì. There are the various subplots and vignettes involving street-sellers, flatmates, children and so on. And then there is Musetta, a skittish character with a penchant for breaking crockery that hints at the presence of Greek blood somewhere in her lineage. The moment where she hurls a plate to the floor is, of course, a potential source of disaster in the orchestra pit, especially on a raked stage. The conductor runs the danger of a shower of plate shards flying towards him, and is advised to wear appropriate protective headwear. It has also been known for the plate not to break, but to roll inexorably across the stage and drop into the pit on to the head of the conductor.

This is possibly the best of all available reasons for the conductor not to bury his head in the score.

So how does the conductor deal with all this? Well, sometimes it's best to set your expectations low and take it from there. So in an opera you should expect to be ignored and work your way upwards.

It begins at the piano rehearsals. Don't think you can have any influence here. The rehearsal pianist has been playing these things for years. She knows what's what. There's no earthly use your charging in with hifalutin ideas about 'doing what the composer wrote' or some such silliness. The whole thing will go quite smoothly without that kind of nonsense, thank you very much.

And then when you get to the stage rehearsals, in comes the director, with ideas and stuff like that. Why not have the soprano sing her final aria swinging upside down from a trapeze? Couldn't the tenor drag her across the stage by her hair during the duet? Wouldn't it be brilliant for the Queen of the Night to sing her famous aria while executing a perfect reproduction of Beth Tweddle's bronze-medal-winning gymnastics routine from the 2012 Olympics?

Your dissenting voice will be swept away on a tide of evangelical zeal. Protestations about practicality, feasibility and even personal safety will amount to nothing. Best save your breath.

No, the only situation where your voice holds any authority is in the *Sitzprobe*. This is the rehearsal where singers and orchestra come together for the first time, unencumbered by the expectations of stagecraft and other such inessentials. Everybody stands still, everybody watches you. You have them at your mercy, so make sure they realise it. Now is the time to be really picky, pedantically rounding on the smallest errors, allowing no corner of the opera to go unexplored. Overtime will be called, tempers will be frayed, muttering will be heard.

In the heat of performance, of course, all your hard work will be forgotten, but at least you'll have had your moment in the sun.

# [24]

# *Teaching*

THERE WILL COME A TIME when you pass from 'wannabe' to 'venerable'. When this moment arrives it behoves the conductor to share his knowledge and experience with those still stuck in the impossible quagmire of Aspirational Conductordom.

Be free with your advice and generous with your time and you will quickly acquire a reputation for 'jolly-good-chappery'.

Used wisely this status can be extremely advantageous.

One way of sharing your hard-earned knowledge, of course, is to teach. Should you be in the fortunate position of acquiring a small teaching practice I hope you will feel moved to share some of the nuggets contained within this text. Whatever happens, you will have your own techniques of pedagogy, and it is in any case a subject worthy of another, even more wide-ranging tome than this.

There is one aspect, however, that may not occur to the new teacher as an important part of the teaching process. I maintain that without it you might as well condemn your unfortunate charges to a life in the slow lane.

## Library Management.

Picture the scene: the young conductor has been invited to the great Maestro's house, maybe for a consultation, perhaps just for an informal mid-morning chat over freshly-ground Turkish coffee and homemade baklava. Either way, you'll want to show him your library. And his first view of the library will be what stays with him, may even be the only thing he remembers of the occasion, so make it impressive.

Everybody's library is different, of course, so let me use a couple of extreme examples to give you some pointers about how best to use the library to convey the right impression.

## 1. The Hectic Library.

The Hectic Library looks as if it has just been ransacked by a particularly single-minded tornado. The room itself isn't huge, and is rather gloomy. A desk and a piano jostle for position at the far end of the room. Heavy curtains add to the sombre, studious air. The room feels serious and knowledgeable but at the same time chaotic and flustered. Scores are piled up on the piano, higgledy-piggledy; they spill off every available surface; a tower of seemingly random (but actually very carefully selected) scores trips the unwary visitor the moment they enter the room; the shelves groan, Eulenburg miniatures of Schubert chamber music mingling with old Russian editions of Kalinnikov symphonies; the desk, if it can be found, is a tsunami of paper, reference books and old cups of coffee.

Preferably, the walls are so full of shelves that there is no space—but closer inspection reveals an atrocious portrait of Beethoven, a signed photograph of Carlos Kleiber and maybe a battered corkboard that overflows with hastily-penned notes urging things like 'Salzburg Mozart—November!', 'Ring Uschi—Seven Early Songs in Adelaide??' or 'Tell Charles Proms or Edinburgh—not both'.

The main light doesn't work. Instead, an old Anglepoise with a broken spring casts a dim pool of light on an area of the desk that is barely suitable for working. The impression is that the conductor's life is so manic that he has to snatch his study whenever he can, bouncing from one project to the next on the helter-skelter treadmill of the modern Maestro.

This impression is, of course, meticulously cultivated. The conductor really does his work in the kitchen with a Dover edition score and a stubby old pencil, consuming cyclopean amounts of instant coffee and Jaffa Cakes as he attempts to cram two hundred and fifty pages of Mahler into his head three months too late. His diary is emptier than a tabloid editor's promise, and the last time he went to Salzburg was on a tour to Mozart's house which yielded a postcard of the composer's harpsichord and a packet of *Mozartkugeln*, both of which still sit in the crowded in-tray under the pile of unpaid bills on his desk.

If the Hectic Library is perfectly arranged, the visiting ingénu will come away with a sore foot, awed respect at your prodigious work rate, and a creeping sense of inadequacy.

Job done.

## 2. The Perfect Library

A shaft of sunlight angles through the shutters, motes of dust cavorting joyously in its beam. There is an air of serenity. In the middle of the room, a Blüthner baby grand, at short stick, Henle edition of Beethoven sonatas open at the *Hammerklavier*; to one side, an elegant *escritoire*, its only adornment either a beautiful antique lamp or, even better, a breathtakingly expensive modern one. ('Salvatore only made a dozen of these—

the quality of light it produces is so conducive to score study'.)

On the desk, a single score, a Faber-Castell 3B (the 'daddy' of pencils), and an artist's eraser. One side of the room is filled, from floor to ceiling, with bespoke shelves which are groaning with scores. These, identically bound in dark green leather, are embossed on the spine with the name of the composer, the title and, with ostentatious modesty, your initials.

It's always a good idea to have a score out on the desk, open to a specifically chosen page. The more complex the score, the better. The page should be meticulously marked with salient pencil markings, conveying the impression of methodical and rigorous work. All the other pages of the score, of course, are completely unmarked, but the student won't see those.

If the student passes comment on the score a throwaway remark such as 'Nico's latest. He always sends me things just to give them the once-over' will suffice to give the impression to the starstruck neophyte that you're a conductor of influence. The truth is that the score is a long-neglected student work written by a breathtakingly incompetent friend of yours who gave it to you as a nineteenth birthday present in the hope that you'd perform it. As it contains parts for twelve Wagner tubas and a chainsaw, the premiere never took place and the composer now works as warehouse manager for his local branch of Staples.

I T HAS TO BE ACKNOWLEDGED that both the above libraries can be costly to build and maintain. Those wishing to create the right impression without the significant investment required for such advanced ploys may wish to consider the third basic library type.

### 3. The Library That Isn't A Library

Comprising no more than a bare room with a pile of cardboard boxes in the corner, this is the easy way out. All you need by way of an explanation is an apologetic 'One day I'll find the time to unpack all my scores', and the impression of a hectic and in-demand conductor will be cemented.

It should go without saying that the boxes need have nothing in them. If you wish to add verisimilitude you may of course have a dozen or so scores on one of the shelves to represent your current activities.

# [25]

# *Rehearsing*

REHEARSAL MANAGEMENT is one of the core crafts of the modern conductor. Time is at such a premium, and yours in particular so expensive, that efficient use of the means available can often be the difference between employment and unemployment, regardless of the actual success of the end result.

But of course it's not as simple as that. Rehearsal efficiency can lead to your work being tarnished with the damning words 'workmanlike', 'organised', and even, horror of horrors, 'competent'.

Of course it's better to be competent than incompetent, but the word 'boring' lurks not far beneath, and that is the true killer.

Far better to be 'frustrating', 'lazy' or 'brilliant but oh so inefficient'. If you're boring, you will always, in the eyes of musicians and management alike, be boring. But if you're touched with what seems like genius, then your future employment is guaranteed.

I use the words 'what seems like genius' because, of course, true genius is within the remit only of the creator, not the recreator. It is possible, however, to convey the impression of absolute brilliance, sometimes with the simplest of methods.

## Selective perfectionism

The art of rehearsing one part of a programme to death, while almost completely neglecting the rest.

Say you're conducting, for example, a Shakespeare programme: Prokofiev's *Romeo and Juliet*, Mendelssohn's *Midsummer Night's Dream*, and so on. Let's also say, for the sake of argument, that you have two days of rehearsal before the concert day.

There's quite a lot of music that needs detailed rehearsal, unpicking the various textures, sorting out balance, going over tricky passagework and so forth. There's also a notoriously difficult and exposed flute solo in the Mendelssohn.

At the beginning of the first rehearsal, play through the Mendelssohn. Then leave it, saying something like 'We'll come to that later'.

You will now not play the Mendelssohn all the way through *until the concert itself.*

This point is crucial.

222

For the rest of the rehearsal period, devote yourself to the pursuit of perfection in one or two (they can be randomly chosen) of the Prokofiev movements. Incidentally, it is now almost routine for conductors to deem the original suites unsatisfactory, and to concoct their own from the available movements. The more switches from one piece of sheet music to another this entails for the players, the better.

It doesn't matter which movement or movements you choose to perfect, but you must spend an inordinate amount of time on the smallest of details, picking out hidden textures, bringing forward unlikely harmonies, fiddling with the balance until everything is to your satisfaction. Correct inaudible bass clarinet tuning; ask for three different triangles to be tried until you hear the one you want; rehearse a single double bass pizzicato until it balances the harp perfectly. That sort of thing. The violins have unplayable passage work in 'The Death of Tybalt'? Top and tail. No more.

Insist that this painstaking approach to what might seem unimportant or simple movements 'lies at the heart of the piece. If they are not just so, everything fails.' As for the notes in the fight scene: 'It is a fight— chaos is in its nature.'

With this you are implying that the musician who cannot see this is somehow at fault, that you and you alone are able to communicate with the soul of the composer. Talk at length about the significance of seemingly insignificant parts in the action of the ballet, and how this relates to the original text. Quote Shakespeare at opportune moments—not the obvious bits, but a single line of the apothecary, say, or even better, something from one of the even more minor characters that nobody has ever heard of, like Gregory or Balthasar.

All the while, the flautist becomes ever more nervous, and practises his Mendelssohn part ever more feverishly. In the concert, he will be fine, having prepared more thoroughly than ever before. And, what's more, the lack of rehearsal will have the players on the edge of their seats, lending the performance a corresponding excitement. The other pieces, having been very thoroughly rehearsed, will also be excellent.

With luck you will get the reputation of a stickler for detail whose attention to the intricacies of the score outweighs any minor administrative headaches that may be caused.

Or everyone will think you're a pompous charlatan with no clue how to organise rehearsal time.

But they probably thought that anyway, so you're really no worse off.

*Rehearsing*

W HILE IT'S POSSIBLE, indeed desirable, to be able to show every nuance of the music with gestures alone, necessity dictates that a conductor speak from time to time. It is here that so many conductors, from greenhorn to grizzled veteran, fall down.

It's important to stress that while what you say does matter, how you say it is even more important. Sometimes you may not even need to speak the same language as the orchestra. I well remember attending the rehearsals for the only London concerts ever given by the great Russian conductor Tchuyaron Legov. He spoke no English, communicating with the orchestra only in mumbled Russian which, even if it had been comprehensible, was only audible to the front desk of violas. Yet the transformation wrought on the orchestra by this titan was simply astounding. Wrestling the music to the ground with his powerful hands, he moulded it to his will, wringing every last drop of meaning from it. His massive frame loomed over the orchestra, yet in this behemoth dwelled supreme sensitivity and an innate understanding of every aspect of the score. His fingers fluttered over the players, delineating the shape of each note, demanding their attention as if he were holding a gun to their heads. When his left elbow quivered, the third horn played quieter. A flick of his chin encouraged the second bassoon to enunciate a true staccato. At one point I could swear I heard a direct correlation between his little finger and the trombone section.

Words were simply not necessary.

At the end of the rehearsal the room burst into spontaneous applause. He silenced us with the slightest motion of his left hand and spoke. I strained to hear, even though I knew I would have no understanding of the actual words, hoping that the great man's insight would be apparent even to non-Russophones.

'Spasibo. V Anglii zhenshchiny vonyayut tukhloi ryboi, i u mushchin nyeznachitelniye penisy. Poshyol na khui vsyo.'

And with that he was gone, his ruddy face wreathed in smiles.

Desperate to understand the meaning of these mysterious syllables, I dashed to the nearest pay phone, repeating them over and over to myself. I called Dmitri, a Russian friend. As accurately as I could, I relayed what the Maestro had said.

'Say it again?'

I repeated the pearls of wisdom.

'Yes,' he said slowly. 'I think Maestro Legov is having some fun at your expense.'

'What do you mean?'

'Well unless you have got it wrong he said 'Thank you. In England the women smell of rotten fish and the men have minuscule penises. Fuck you all.'

*Rehearsing*

WHILE MAESTRO LEGOV was a rare exception, the lesson is clear. Use words sparingly. And when you do use them, make them count.

Opinion is divided on how best to achieve this. There are those who deal only with baldly factual statements.

'Two before B, trumpets, play quieter. Five after C, violas were behind. Ten before D, first flute was sharp...'

While this may seem the most efficient way of doing things, the conductor risks losing the interest of the orchestra, who, like anyone else, want to be inspired.

The other extreme is little better.

'This symphony is like a six-course meal: the stark simplicity of the hors d'œuvre, the understated elegance of the fish course, the daintiness of the *"trou normand"*, the robust and chewy earthiness of the main course, the pungency associated with a fine blue cheese, and finally the silky luxuriance of the pudding. We must make the audience salivate.'

All very entertaining if you like that kind of thing, but uninformative to the point of secrecy.

Perhaps the best approach is a combination of the two.

'Please, play this louder. In a mushroomy way.'

'This chord must be truly noxious, but still *pianissimo*.'

'Play this as if stroking a cat's ears, but don't let it be flat in the lower register.'

'This phrase is like a glass of 1961 Château Haut-Brion. We shouldn't want it to end. But make sure you drain the glass. With vibrato.'

And so on.

Remember: when it comes to orchestras, if they're sleepin', you're weepin'.

# [26]

# *Listening*

A CONDUCTOR'S LIFE IS A TOUGH ONE.
It's well known that most orchestras have made up their mind about a conductor within five seconds of the poor fool stepping up to the podium.

In some cases, even sooner.

The conductor must therefore possess a hide like an elephant, albeit one elegantly clothed in a soft cashmere polo neck by Hugo Boss. He must also be prepared to fight back.

There are of course many ways in which a conductor can hurt an orchestra, either intentionally or otherwise, but not all of them are practical, and those that are may not be strictly ethical or even legal. Subtlety must be your watchword. With a series of small psychological gambits it is possible to sow the seed of doubt that will eventually bear the most abundant fruit: your mastery of the orchestra.

A basic but very effective ploy is what one might term 'Competitive Listening'. Use it wisely, and you can give the orchestra the impression that you'll hear every mistake they make, no matter how tiny.

Proceed, however, with caution. No matter how much you might want them to be, orchestral players aren't total morons.

Super-Aural Ploys are numerous. Here are some of the simplest.

Example 1: The Balance Barometer. In the middle of any passage in which the whole orchestra plays, start looking meaningfully at the brass. In the unlikely event that they start playing more quietly, give them another, encouraging, look, as if they're being too sensitive. When they start playing much louder, shush them impatiently as if you can no longer bear their appalling unmusicality. Finally, stop, shake your head, and say in tones of exaggerated patience, 'Ladies and gentlemen, it's really very simple—we must *listen* to each other.'

Example 2: There is a passage in which several woodwind instruments play a unison line. Pick the least penetrating of them, and exaggeratedly encourage them. No matter how loudly they end up playing, stop and spend the next fifteen minutes adjusting the balance of one note until it is just how you like it. Obviously it doesn't really matter what it sounds like—

you just want to give them the impression that you can hear things nobody else can.

Example 3: In one of the complex passages in, say, a tone poem of Richard Strauss, insist that an accidental is wrong. This will, preferably, mean the amendment of several parts, at some inconvenience to the players involved (changing a D sharp, for example, to a D double sharp). Insist that 'He couldn't possibly have meant that', with a pityingly indulgent smile for the poor saps whose harmonic understanding is so rudimentary that they could entertain the notion that a D sharp was the right note. N.B. The shorter and more fleeting the note in question, and the more hidden in the texture, the better.

Example 4: Announce, at the first rehearsal, 'Ladies and gentlemen, we will of course play the original version at letter M.' You know perfectly well that there isn't (and never has been) an alternative version, but the implication of your superior knowledge will have been ever so subtly implanted in the players' minds.

As well as these, and myriad variations thereto, it goes without saying that in the general rehearsal you will unveil the most basic technique of them all. When you reach a section that is particularly awkward to negotiate, jump off the podium and go into the body of the hall 'to listen to the balance'. Those versed in orchestral practice will know that this can often result in the players listening to each other more than when they have the 'safety net' of the conductor in front of them, with a concomitant improvement in the quality of sound, ensemble and general musical awareness.

But if you've chosen the passage well, and ensured that it is rhythmically or texturally fragile, it will, in all likelihood, stutter or wobble. It may even fall apart altogether. It's up to you whether, on returning to the podium, you pass comment on the balance—this aspect of the ploy is almost irrelevant. The point is that the orchestra will, against years of experience and their better judgement, subliminally feel that they need you.

It has to be said, however, that this ploy does run the danger of backfiring unless you're actually able to conduct the passage in question in such a way that it's improved by your presence.

The techniques outlined above form the basis of any conductor's listening strategy. It is, of course, entirely possible that the use of any or all of these tactics could result in a seething vat of poisonous bile coming in your direction from the frustrated and downtrodden players, but you must stick to your guns. They hated you already, right? What can you lose?

# [27]

# *Anecdotes*

AS YOUR STUDIES CONTINUE and you gradually absorb the many intricacies of the conductor's craft, you will reach the stage where, on a clear day and with the wind behind you, as it were, you will be able to stand in front of an orchestra during their rendition of any piece from the standard repertoire, and (modestly, of course) take the credit for it.

But none of the blame, obviously.

But we mustn't get ahead of ourselves. It's all very well learning how to wave your Versace-clad arms in time to an orchestra like some trained monkey (albeit a beautifully-coiffured, well-dressed and highly-paid one), but a performance without rehearsal is, like a fifteen-round naked mud-wrestling contest between Ed Miliband and David Cameron, something most sane people would prefer not to witness.

We've already examined many aspects of the conductor's rôle, but in truth we've only scratched the surface. What of intellectual rigour? The many hours of painstaking preparation? The stripping away of layer after layer of musical detail until the beating heart of the music is laid bare? The fine honing that enables the audience to hear the composer's true voice in all its plain and unvarnished glory? The unwavering adherence to the gruelling and endless quest for musical honesty?

Well, frankly, what of them?

They're fine and dandy if you like that kind of thing, and might have their place in some rarefied utopian über-universe, but in the grim world of Real Life and Hard Knocks, what you really need in rehearsal is a good supply of anecdotes.

Never mind aural expertise, pish and tish to realising the overall vision of the composer, bah humbug to conveying hidden meaning.

Anecdotes are where it's at.

It's crucial, however, to grasp the underlying principles before attempting to tell an anecdote in rehearsal. Here are some guidelines.


Familiarity

When telling an anecdote about great musical figures of the past, you must somehow convey the impression

234

that you knew them, even if they died thirty or more years before you were born. Good standbys are 'Klemps', 'Timber', 'Lenny', 'Stokie' and so on. Practical examples include: 'Of course Klemps wasn't as fierce as he made out', 'Aah, Lenny—what a man. There was that time in Boston...', and 'So then old Stokie said, in that unmistakeable voice of his...'.

### Aptness
Don't make them too technical. If an anecdote begins 'The funny thing about the Tristan Chord is...', you're losing at least half your audience before you start.

### Accents
If attempting to impersonate a foreign conductor, your accent must either be perfect or deliberately and comically atrocious.

### Timing
Fairly obvious, this. Neither start nor finish your rehearsal with an anecdote. Rather, choose a moment when you sense that the orchestra may have reached the end of their tether. If it interrupts a crucial discussion about bowings, or delays the coffee break by fifteen minutes or so, what of it? The important thing is to show what a Jolly Good Chap you are underneath it all. The orchestra will laugh because they have to, your

ego will feel appropriately pampered, and the fact that the crucial transition to the finale went unrehearsed will merely lend that important extra spark come performance time.

Everyone wins.

# [28]

# *Props*

WE'VE ALREADY TALKED about the importance of clothing for the aspiring conductor. But it would be a mistake to think that once you are fully clothed the job is done.

You should always be thinking of ways to enhance your appearance and image, whether it's by the addition of memorable facial hair, employment of a blatantly desirable personal assistant, or judicious use of accessories.

Accessories (or 'props') can take many forms, from the towel casually slung over the shoulder to the battered leather briefcase (most effective, incidentally, if bearing someone else's initials entirely). Each one serves a purpose, playing a small but vital rôle in the building of a persona. It is often through imaginative deployment of props that a conductor can make a significant breakthrough in his relationship with an orchestra.

Let us deal with clothing accessories first.

## Spectacles

Very standard. Try to aim for a distinctive spectacle technique. Options include:

1. Wearing them on your head at all times. It's essential, if choosing this option, that you never actually use them. The more adventurous will take this technique to its logical conclusion and wear them on their head *even in concert.*

2. Tucking them into the neck of your shirt. Rather bland, this option, but there's always the possibility of enlivening it by never being able to remember where you've put them. (A variation is of course to wear them on a string round your neck 'because I'm always losing them', and then constantly forgetting that you have them on a string round your neck.)

3. Keeping them in some other eccentric place, the more ridiculous the better. One of the great spectaclesmen (although an atrocious conductor) was undoubtedly Sir Huxtable Nimby—he wrote an enlightening pamphlet on 'Spectacles Storage for the Modern Conductor', which specified no fewer than forty-three distinct places for keeping a pair of glasses about the person, including in the socks, down the

pants, and tucked into the epaulettes of a particular design of Brooks Brothers shirt.

4. Conducting with them instead of a baton. Use sparingly.

Wherever you keep them, they're of tremendous use when you're asked a question by one of the musicians. A standard ploy is as follows: take them out, put them on to examine the place in the score (you needn't be looking at the actual place, of course), suck pensively on them, then nod curtly before delivering your answer.

## Gloves

Quite rare nowadays, a well-wielded pair of gauntlets used to be standard equipment for a certain school of British conductor. They would, of course, be rarely worn, but more often used as a key 'Moment of Arrival' prop, the conductor wielding them with a carefree flourish as they entered the rehearsal hall, along with a silver-topped cane, cashmere overcoat and grey Homburg hat.

Usual practice was to dispense with them for the rehearsal, leaving them ostentatiously on a chair with the hat and cane. Ansty Cowfold was the pioneer of the golfer's 'glove hanging out of back pocket' look. Although he persevered with it for a few years, it never gained traction in the conducting community, possibly because it served no discernible purpose whatsoever.

More radical was Hector Winslow-Munderfield's habit of wearing a pair of white gloves while conducting. At first thought stunningly original, this proved within a short space of time to be a disastrous ploy. Not only did it make him look like a snooker referee, but he failed to practise turning pages with the gloves, with the result that in the middle of a performance of Tchaikovsky's First Symphony he skipped from the fast and nimble scherzo to the lugubrious introduction to the last movement. His efforts to find his place again meant that he stopped conducting almost entirely, instead flapping his hand pathetically above his head, as if to say 'Go on without me'.

The orchestra, accustomed to ignoring him, were only too happy to oblige.

## Jewellery

While perfectly acceptable for women, jewellery has no place in the male conductor's ensemble.

Just don't. Really.

## Handkerchiefs

Indispensable, whether for mopping your brow during a particularly strenuous rehearsal or to buy yourself time when a player asks an awkward question.

*Props*

A white handkerchief can also be usefully employed to defuse tensions in rehearsal. Simply wave it at the brass in a gesture of surrender. It's sure to get a laugh—whether in sympathy or scorn, you'll never know, but a laugh's a laugh.

## Odd socks

I must make mention of the eccentric, but mysteriously effective, use of socks by Latvian Maestro Griva Ziedonis. He was a stickler for appearance, and was always impeccably turned out, with one glaring exception. It was his habit in rehearsal always to wear a pair of odd socks of wildly ill-matched colours—shocking pink and lime green, for example, or sky blue and burgundy. They would be beautiful and fine socks, for sure, but invariably odd.

Reaction to the socks would vary. If nobody mentioned it, then fine, the rehearsal proceeded as usual. Sometimes there would be giggling in the orchestra, which he pretended not to notice. Once in a while, however, someone would say something along the lines of, 'Er, excuse me, Maestro, but are you aware that you're wearing odd socks?'

Eschewing the hackneyed Klemperer response 'And vot hass zat got to do viz Beethoven?' Ziedonis leaned forward and asked the musician to repeat himself.

'Your socks, Maestro. They're of differing colours.'

Slowly, and with a shocked look in his eye as of one who has realised that something somewhere has gone terribly wrong, Ziedonis would look down at his feet. Taking in the sight of his socks, he would pale slightly and mutter a horrified 'Oh no' under his breath. He would then sit, frozen, for a few seconds, perhaps shaking his head in silent disbelief, before addressing the orchestra. Sometimes he would clasp his hands together beseechingly.

'Ladies and gentlemen, I owe you an apology. The conductor should pay his orchestra the courtesy of impeccable clothing at all times. I have failed in my duty. However, with your permission, we will continue as best we can.'

Reaction to this varied: sometimes the musicians struggled to stifle giggles; on other occasions there was a bemused silence. Invariably, though, the orchestra was placed on the back foot.

Ziedonis's usual practice at this point was to attempt to continue the rehearsal. But he was now in a sombre mood, unable to concentrate, and easily distracted. After ten minutes or so, he would lay down his stick and ask if, with the orchestra's indulgence, they could take a short unscheduled break so that he could regain his composure.

*Props*

After the break he would return, but (and I can never work out whether this is the important bit or not), clothed from head to toe in black.

His mood restored, the rehearsal would then continue as normal.

This is without doubt, and up against some pretty stiff competition, the most eccentric example of conductorial behaviour I have ever heard of. It would be easy to dismiss it as mere whimsy, or inconsequential eccentricity, and nothing to do with the art of conducting. Easy, but mistaken.

The fact is, every orchestral musician I've ever spoken to who worked with Ziedonis has told a version of this story, and the end is always the same: 'That evening we gave the best performance any of us can remember. Don't ask me how or why.'

The power of the Maestro is sometimes mysterious and unfathomable.


Other props:
Baton case
There are two options if you want to stand out:

1. A truly luxurious and noble baton case, solid oak, with purple velvet lining, and niches for different sized batons as well as pencils and other accoutrements, out of which you take a wilted excuse for a stick with a broken tip.

2. A Lidl plastic bag carrying at least two dozen sticks of differing dimensions and a shabby pocket score of the piece you're conducting.

## Pencils

The well-chosen pencil can say volumes about the kind of conductor you are. If cultivating the image of The Aesthete, then you must be pernickety about them, insisting that you use 'only 3B, and NEVER Staedtler—they smear in hot conditions. No, I'm afraid I've always been a Faber-Castell man.' At the other end of the spectrum, The Whirlwind conductor will most often not have a pencil at all, but will grab the nearest thing handy; or will make a great show of looking for a pencil in his case before producing a grubby stump of a thing with flattened lead with which they scrawl 'TEMPO!' in wild letters across the page, and which they then use as a makeshift baton for the rest of the rehearsal.

BEYOND THE PROPS already mentioned, you should be aware of isolated examples of 'eccentric proppery', all of which had their own effect in the hands of their users:

## Props

The small silver trophy (Sir Huxtable Nimby). It was no more than eight inches tall, and rarely came out of his briefcase, but he would on occasion adorn his dressing room mantelpiece with it prior to inviting carefully selected orchestra members in on the pretext of discussing their part in the third movement. It was a standard, non-specific trophy of the kind often awarded by a snooker or golf club. On closer inspection it was possible to discern the words 'Man of the Year 1935' on the tarnished brass plaque that adorned it.

Toy car. Royston Malpas-Oldcastle would always have his 'lucky Bentley' on his music stand. It was a beautiful model, to be sure, but would on occasion cause problems due to his wild page-turning technique. On more than one occasion he sent it flying towards the front desk of the first violins.

Gaston l'Houche-Poupée, the master of the laid-back style of conducting, used a yoyo to great effect. He would idly play with it while conducting a rehearsal. The genius of this technique lay in his ability to keep the yoyo going at a completely different speed from his right hand, with which he was conducting. I also once saw him conduct a rehearsal with the yoyo while perched on a high stool chewing gum and reading a Spiderman comic, but this was a less successful technique.

# MUSICAL ASPECTS

# [29]

# *The Instruments*

YOU DON'T NEED ME TO TELL YOU the properties of all the different instruments in the orchestra. It's not that I'm assuming any knowledge on your part, merely that the information is so freely available elsewhere that it would be a waste of my time and the world's paper (or pixels, depending on which version you're reading) to do so.

So if you're after the lowest note on a piccolo (D), the highest on an oboe (A, but you don't want to be sitting next to it), or the difference between a tamtam and a tom-tom (do you really need to ask?), then may I direct you to the multi-faceted resource pioneered by Sir Timothy Berners-Lee in the late 1980s?

If you don't know who Sir Timothy Berners-Lee is, then may I direct you to the multi-faceted resource pioneered by...

Oh.

Anyway, instruments.

What you really want to know is 'How much do I need to know? Is it really necessary to spend all that time learning about the instruments? Isn't that the job of the players? I've got enough on my plate with all this arm-waving business without worrying about how difficult things are for the third horn or how many keys a flute's got. Leave all that to the specialists. After all, the CEO of a car manufacturer doesn't need to know how to strip down an engine, does he?'

Nor he does.

It's also true that a little knowledge can be a dangerous thing, as any non-string-playing conductor who has ever suggested a fingering to a violinist can attest.

So rather than embark on an exhaustive list of all the individual pitfalls to avoid, most of which will be situation-specific in any case, I merely present a short list of 'Golden Rules' for the aspiring conductor. Stick to these and you won't go far wrong.

1. String players love to talk about bowings. Indulge them. While the discussion is under way, you can always treat the rest of the orchestra to a mini-break in Paris. They'll still be going when you come back.

2. Sorting out wind tuning is almost as much fun as discussing bowings. Invite contributions from the other members of the orchestra to show you're open and

democratic. You're bound to reach a consensus soon enough.

3. Brass players are always keen to hone their rest-counting skills. Help them in this endeavour: play a passage in which they're not involved, and stop to rehearse the strings just before their entry. They will appreciate your thoughtfulness.

4. Oboists are always keen to improve the timbre of their instrument. Help them achieve this goal by regularly asking them to 'Play this passage more like a clarinet'.

5. It's easy to forget that timpanists need attention too. A request for 'harder sticks' will make them feel involved in the rehearsal process.

6. Sitting in an orchestra can be tiring, and it's important that players remain as flexible as possible. A simple group exercise can help this: make as if to start a passage involving the whole orchestra, then tell a short anecdote while the players have their instruments up and ready to play; at the end of the anecdote, allow them to lower their instruments while you make a point about articulation; repeat.

# [30]

# *Programming*

RARE, AND FRANKLY LAUGHABLE, is the conductor who doesn't have strong ideas about programming. There still remains, however, the vexed question of balance. It's all too easy to assume that whatever you dish up the audience will devour it like a ravening Droolbeast as long as you include some Vivaldi with it.

But it's a lot more complicated than that. When it comes to the public's taste, there are subtleties at play beyond the realms of quality, fashion and whimsy.

There's a lot in a name. Try to avoid composers whose names include more than two of the following letters: c, j, k, w, x, y, z. So Wagner is fine, obviously; likewise Bruckner, Mozart, Bach, Vivaldi and legions of similarly unthreateningly-named composers of all eras. But Mieczysław Karłowicz, Joonas Kokkonen, or Stanisław Skrowaczewski? Sorry. No matter which way you slice them, these names scream 'My music is incredibly intense and difficult and your brain is going to hurt after two minutes. Avoid at all costs.' Reality is irrelevant. It wouldn't matter if they wrote a piece called *'The Simplest and Most Unthreateningly Hummable Tunes of All Time'*—people would still think it was 'difficult'.

John Adams, on the other hand, is a name that exudes solidity, ordinary-blokery and trustworthiness. And the titles of his pieces are cunningly chosen. Why does *Short Ride In A Fast Machine* receive so many performances? It's all in the title. Even the most untrusting of audiences will warm to it, and all because of that first word. 'Short'. On seeing that word, the potential audience thinks 'It's ok. Whatever cacophony will be assaulting our ears, at least it'll be over in less than five minutes. Says so in the title.'

*The Chairman Dances* is doubly subtle. The downtrodden worker, even if he or she is unaware of the nuances of world politics in the 1970s, will be drawn to the title. The chairman dances? It may not be 'The CEO Sings Karaoke', but any hint of the humiliation of anyone higher up on the corporate ladder than you has got to be worth a listen, right?

Contrast this with Lutosławski's *Chain 3*, a piece whose name could have been chosen by the 'Random Impenetrable Contemporary Music Name Generator'.

What's in a name? Everything.

# [31]

# *Composers*

AS IN THE 'INSTRUMENTS' CHAPTER, rather than forcing you to plough through an encyclopædic listing of how to conduct individual composers or pieces of music, this section is more of a guide with which I hope to temper your own personal preferences. It's based on many years of experience—if there's a trap out there into which I haven't fallen, I don't know of it, so I hope this chapter will help you avoid the most egregious of your inevitable and numerous mistakes.

Bach
Acquire a large brain.
Surround yourself with wonderful musicians.
Try not to slow anything down.
Do as little as possible.
Come to think of it, this applies to all composers.

## Haydn

Haydn is the dark chocolate of 18th-century composers. By conducting his music, and especially by doing so in preference to Mozart, you are automatically establishing yourself as 'a cut above'.

When pressed on the subject, your response should be on the lines of 'Well of course, anyone can love Mozart, but...well, there's everything in Haydn.'

To illustrate this, point to a passage in one of the symphonies that nobody knows (there are plenty to choose from), smile with a glint of mischief in your eyes, and raise an eyebrow as if to say 'You see?' Your interlocutor will have no choice but to agree lest he appear an ignoramus. It should go without saying that the more mundane the passage you're enthusing about, the better.

But it doesn't go without saying. That's why I've said it.

## Mozart

The main problem with conducting Mozart isn't actually the conducting of Mozart; it's the non-conducting of Mozart.

Let me explain.

Here is a typical conversation between the Delusional Innocent Conductor (that's you) and the Worldly Advice Giver (that's anyone who has conducted more concerts than you, and even plenty who haven't).

Delusional Innocent Conductor: I don't suppose you'd be interested in coming to my concert?

Worldly Advice Giver: (slightly wary) What are you playing?

DIC: I'm conducting, actually. It's in aid of Worthy Charity. I've got Slightly-Respected Violinist to play K219. *Linz* symphony in the second half. *Figaro* overture.

WAG: (sharp intake of breath) Brave choice.

DIC: (flustered) What? How do you mean?

WAG: Well of course, if you've got the players...I'm sure it'll be fine...but...well, Mozart...so terribly hard. For everyone, not least the conductor.

DIC: (not sure) Oh...yes, I know what you mean...

WAG: Nowhere to hide, you see.

DIC: Quite. (Pause) I mean, I've got some very good players...and of course Slightly-Respected Violinist is terribly good...and, well, you know...Mozart.

WAG: (reassuring) Oh quite, I don't mean to...I heard her Tchaikovsky. Very...muscular.

DIC: Muscular? I wouldn't say she was...

WAG: Just a bit...(jabs the air) you know. Of course, Mozart needs such a delicate touch.

DIC: Absolutely.

WAG: But not weak. Never weak.

DIC: Of course not.

(Pause)

WAG: Really, of course, the best thing to do in Mozart is nothing at all. (Laughs). But even that's harder than it looks!

DIC: (totally uncertain now) Yes...I suppose so...

Completely undermined, the Delusional Innocent Conductor (that's you) changes the programme to one of all-Russian music. The extra players and instrument hire cost over a thousand pounds, an outlay that you underwrite personally. Worthy Charity receives £37.47.

Beethoven

Impossible.

What are you going to bring to this composer? It's all been done before.

Extremely slow tempi? Klemperer etc.

Extremely fast tempi? Norrington etc.

Everything else in between? Everyone else in between.

Cut your losses. Do something else.

Brahms

The Brahms conductor is cultured, with passion and intellect held in perfect balance. Overdo it in the histrionics department, and you'll be dismissed as a charlatan. But if you bring too much of an intellectual approach you'll be accused of 'lacking warmth' or 'failing to understand the true heart of Brahms.'

Basically, you can't win.

You'll almost certainly, however, find yourself asked to conduct some of his music at one point or another, so it's a good idea to have some notion of how to approach it.

If you have a fondness for rubato, you'll be tempted to indulge it to an almost nauseating degree. Resist this temptation—save that kind of thing for Mahler.

If, on the other hand, you favour an approach that is somewhat lacking in flexibility, perhaps your particular skill set will be more suited to Stravinsky.

And if you feel yourself to be a True Brahmsian, it's best not to advertise this. Membership of the 'True Brahmsian' Club closed years ago.

As with all composers, it's not a bad idea to be armed with things to say:

'Of course, the trombone writing in Brahms is second to none.'

'The triangle! Where is the triangle?'

'Please, ladies and gentlemen, the sound must glow with the warmth of an autumn sun.'

'This moment...it is...well, one can only say "Pure Brahms".'

## Wagner

No composer divides music lovers like Wagner.

For some, he's the single most important figure in the history of music: part revolutionary, part visionary, all genius. His conception of *Gesamtkunstwerk*, his radical use of chromatic harmony, Leitmotifs and tonal extremism, his overwhelming imagination, his reinvention of both opera and the orchestra—it's simply not possible to ignore the far-reaching influence of this great man. And the music—ah, the music! To hear Wagner is to enter the realms of ecstasy—he created a fantastical sound world in which it is possible to lose oneself over and over again, a universe of boundless invention whose myriad delights reward a lifetime's exploration.

For others, he's just a great big anti-Semitic bore.

If you have even a little toe dangling in the pool of cynicism represented by the latter statement, then conducting his music is probably not for you. Rather, set yourself to one side, and with all modesty proclaim 'there are some composers whose music I will never be ready to conduct'—a statement which can be taken either way.

If you're in the former camp, you will already have formed your own opinions, and will need no guidance from me, except perhaps towards a good stockist of sandals in the Floral Street area.

## Tchaikovsky

A conductor's delight, but exhausting. There are almost literally endless opportunities for ecstatic thrashing, few of which you'll want to pass up.

Be careful, though, not to overthrash too early on. Tchaikovsky's penchant for repetition will leave you nowhere to go, not to mention absolutely spent, if you expend all your energy and passion early on in the movement. In any case it's always a good idea to have an energy drink to hand, as well as the phone number of a good osteopath.

## Berlioz

Occupying a small corner of the repertoire to himself, with a purple neon sign above it saying 'Bonkers', Hector Berlioz is a conductor's dream. Wildly extravagant gestures, hysterical tempi, grotesque rubato—anything goes.

If your inner purist complains, shush him and point him in the direction of the following, from the score of Berlioz's own *Grande Messe des Morts*: 'The number [of performers] indicated is only relative. If space permits, the chorus may be doubled or tripled, and the orchestra be proportionally increased. But in the event of an exceptionally large chorus, say seven to eight hundred voices, the entire chorus should only be used for the *Dies Irae*, the *Tuba Mirum*, and the *Lacrymosa*, the rest of the movements being restricted to four hundred voices.'

'Restricted to four hundred voices.'

There speaks a man who is no stranger to extremes. You think he's going to complain if you go over the top?

Bruckner

To conduct Bruckner you will require:

1. A flawless and profound understanding of the architecture of the particular piece you're conducting;

2. An innate ability to draw out both the micro (individual details as small and crucial as the leaves on a tree) and the macro (the overarching structure of a vast cathedral-like musical form);

3. A strong bladder.

Elgar

It's tempting to say that all you need to conduct Elgar is a bushy moustache, a tweed suit and an upper lip trembling with repressed emotion. Stand still, salute, and away you go.

But of course his music isn't all about the famous marches and the *Enigma Variations*, and there are passages of great difficulty. Above all, an understanding of structure is essential, as is an innate feeling for the particular sound world inhabited by this most English of composers.

A bushy moustache won't do you any harm, though.

Stravinsky
You'll be tempted to display your wares by attempting *The Rite of Spring*.

Do not do this.

We have become so used to the perfection of this piece in recent years, and it has become so ubiquitous, that nothing is to be gained by your paltry efforts.

Feel free, however, to refer to it as often as you like when rehearsing other pieces, no matter who wrote them (although you might be hard pressed to link it to an early Haydn symphony). 'Seminal', 'still sounds contemporary', 'far-reaching influence', blah blah blah. All good solid irrefutable stuff.

Likewise, the difficulties of those conductor-magnets *Petrushka* and *The Firebird* make them high-maintenance pieces for the ambitious neophyte.

No, if you're going to conduct any Stravinsky, make it one of the lesser-known pieces: *Orpheus*, *Zvezdolikiy*, the *Aldous Huxley Variations*. Never mind the quality of the music, nor the disaster at the box office—feel the width of your repertoire. You'll be showing an original and creative spirit, and can always make up for it with a Film Music concert to bring the punters in.

When it comes to the actual conducting, you'll need ample reference to the short passage on beating patterns (see p.157) if the whole thing is not to collapse in a welter of increasingly desperate and arrhythmic thrashing. Resist the temptation to explain in advance whether you're beating 5/8 bars in 2+3 or 3+2, and other such irrelevances. Let them work it out for themselves, and make it absolutely clear that if they can't do this by watching carefully, it's their fault not yours.

## Sibelius

Swans, forests, lakes, nationalism, originality.

That should do you.

## Shostakovich

With most composers, the conductor is able to give musical instructions without the added complication of having to know, and identify with at some deep inner level, every detail of the composer's life.

Would that this were so with Shostakovich.

So dramatic were the conditions in which he lived, and so vivid his musical palette, that it's now almost compulsory for any conductor worth his salt to invoke historical context in Shostakovich, no matter how flimsy or tangential the evidence. A few examples:

Loud marching music—empty triumph, mockery of Stalin.

Tragic and hushed music—the downtrodden people, voiceless, disenfranchised, praying for their motherland.

Snare drum—machine gun.

Thumping timpani—the bombastic tyrant Stalin.

Motor rhythm—the inhuman machine of the state.

Any cheerful or jaunty music—not really cheerful or jaunty, cocking a snook at authority, hidden sorrow, wearing the mask etc.

High bassoon solo—the lone flickering candle.

No matter how true all of this is, it has become trite and clichéd, and must stop. Rather, when Shostakovich writes *pp*, merely say 'Ladies and gentlemen, when Shostakovich asks for a *pianissimo*, it has a special significance...(leave a gap here to give extra emphasis to your words)...he means...play very quietly.'

## Mahler

And so we come back to where we started.

Mahler is, from opening shudder to closing grunt, the conductor's composer.

Conduct him like Bruckner, but with added histrionics.

# Conclusion

S O WHAT ARE WE TO MAKE OF ALL THIS?

At the beginning of the book I wrote 'If you learn just one thing from this book, whether it be the best speed for *Nimrod* when played in a muddy field outside Saffron Walden or the correct amount to tip a stage-door Johnny in Caracas, I will have, in part at least, fulfilled my duty.'

Oh dear.

The perceptive reader will have noted, with a disappointed 'Tsk', my neglect of those burning issues. And they lead me to a confession. Two, actually.

Confession No. 1: I've never conducted Elgar's *Enigma Variations* in a muddy field in Saffron Walden (nor in fact in any kind of outdoor arena anywhere).

Confession No. 2: I've never been to Caracas.

These facts therefore render me ill equipped to supply you with advice.

My cheeks should burn with shame at these confessions, evidence as they are that you've been lured through this book on a false promise. I offered you information and didn't deliver. Worse, by continuing to withhold these titbits I am effectively cocking you a snook and running away.

You've been duped, conned, hoaxed, diddled, bamboozled, hoodwinked and led up the garden path.

As I say, my cheeks should burn with shame.

But they don't, for one simple reason.

I am a conductor.

In any case, if you've been paying attention you should, whether or not you actually know the answers, at least be able to come up with plausible ones.

Nunc est dirigendum!

# Acknowledgements

THIS BOOK WOULD HAVE BEEN in much worse shape had it not been for the calm professionalism of my editor Keith Clarke—any mistakes are mine, not his. Ida Miller was also invaluable in winkling out dodgy spellings, misguided punctuation and well-meaning but muddle-headed usages. I don't know whether my beta readers actually enjoyed reading the various versions of the book that were sent to them, but they gave their time freely and willingly and said all the right things. They are: Pamela Brown, Christopher Gillett, John and Sally Isaacs, Amos Miller (who also gave me Yonatan Büsser-Staud), Paul Moylan and Toby Purser. Andrew Brown of Design for Writers designed the cover—he's jolly nice and a brilliant designer. My late mother, Diana Parikian, read the original articles and other early jottings and provided dutiful and, I think, sincere praise. And finally, no list of acknowledgements would be complete without mentioning the unflinching support of my wife and son, Tessa and Olli, into whose lives the writing of this book has intruded unduly. They bear my increasingly lunatic babblings with great patience.

If you have enjoyed this book, do visit www.runnythoughts.com and follow @levparikian & @etwasruhiger on Twitter.

Thank you.

7211372R00170

Printed in Great Britain
by Amazon.co.uk, Ltd.,
Marston Gate.